Strange But True, Colorado

STRANGE BUT TRUE, COLORADO

Weird Tales of the Wild West

By
John Hafnor

Illustrated
By
Dale Crawford

**Lone Pine
Productions**

Fort Collins, Colorado

Library of Congress Control Number: 2005920850

ISBN+10   0-964-8175-3-5
ISBN+13   978-0-964-8175-3-1
Manufactured in the United States of America

Published by Lone Pine Productions
Distribution and Marketing: Attn: John Hafnor, Lone Pine Productions, 4900 Lone Pine Drive, Fort Collins, Colorado 80526-4708 Phone (970) 223-2747. Email jhafnor@aol.com

Book editor, John Hughes, Fort Collins, CO

Cover Design: Designs by Andrew (andylock@frii.com).
Book Design: Old Army Press (oldarmypress@msn.com).

Discover unpublished stories at **www.strangecolorado.com**

To Fran, for choosing me over a rich guy.

Dale Crawford

To Adam, Joel, Andrew-

And the gift of seeing boys become men.

John Hafnor

Contents

Words from the Illustrator

The American West has fascinated me from my earliest memories. This may seem odd, considering that I grew up in Wisconsin. But then, most everyone who settled the West came from "back East" somewhere. I can't fully explain it, but I do feel like I was born 100 years too late!

My other love was, and still is, art. I can not remember a time when I didn't draw. And I feel blessed to be able to earn a living doing something that I truly love.

Over many years of working as a graphic artist, I've had the opportunity to create many illustrations for a variety of clients. But the drawings I loved the most were invariably associated with the Old West. In 1973, after our daughter had completed kindergarten, Fran and I moved to Colorado. This trek completed a dream we had thought about for several years.

I began work at a Colorado ad agency as their graphic artist. During the first year, I chanced to meet book publisher Mike Koury, who specialized in Old West themes, especially Custer and the military. Thus began my side career as a book illustrator. In my heart, I don't believe this would have happened if we had not pulled up stakes and moved out West.

We had taken a chance in moving. Had we known how bad the economy really was, we might not have moved then—or perhaps ever! As it was, we left family, friends, jobs and a home to start over. It was in some ways reminiscent of the westward-bound frontier families, except that we came in a Chevy Nova, not a covered wagon!

For those first two years in Colorado, I continued to work full-time as a graphic artist for local and regional clients while illustrating stories and books as a freelance artist on the side.

But 1975 found me without a regular job. I decided to open my own graphic design business, and have continued it to this day. In 1976, Mike Koury introduced me to Don Rickey, an author looking for an artist to illustrate his latest book. Rickey's first book, on the frontier military, was *Forty Miles a Day on Beans and Hay*. He was now tackling the formidable subject of cowboys of the 1880s. I jumped at this chance. The book, *$10 Horse, $40 Saddle*, became a classic among those with interest in cowboy lore. I created over 100 pen-and-ink illustrations of authentic cowboy guns, clothing, equipment and horse gear. I not only enjoyed the job, but learned a lot in the process. This project made me realize my initial interest in all things Western was not the "real" West, but the "reel" West of the matinees and television of the 1950s.

Growing up, Roy Rogers was my hero. But I would go to any Western movie, no matter who the star was. I'm still the same way today. Anyone who cares to look back at my earliest grade school pictures can see the western influence in my dress even then—cowboy belt buckles, pinto colored cowboy shirts, and more. Almost every family photo shows me with my favorite cap pistols strapped to my sides.

I can remember the first cowboy boots my dad got for me—and I can still smell the leather and see that multi-colored stitching. Yup, you can say that I'm hooked on the West. Young boys of my generation may have fallen in love with a West that never was, but in this modern world wouldn't it be nice to tell the good guy from the bad guy simply by the color of his hat?

Of course, we can't go back to the 1950s. But we can travel anywhere we wish just by opening a book. The history of our region is so rich, varied and vast that you can be assured of finding your area of interest. Isn't that part of the reason why you picked up this book?

Do you realize how young the history of our country is? Wyatt Earp did not pass away until 1929. His common law wife Josephine lived until 1944, the year of my birth. Don Rickey was able to interview several old cowboys in the 1950s, men who had been in their prime in the 1880s—a rare last chance to interview, firsthand, the fabled frontier cowpoke. It wasn't until 1956 that the last Civil War soldier died. All this should remind us that when we are reading America's history, it is all pretty darn new and we are closer to it than we think.

I met John Hafnor through—you guessed it—Mike Koury, the man who has introduced me to so many other authors over the years. John presented the idea of a unique book, and it sounded very interesting to me. We struck a deal on a handshake—he would furnish the short stories and I would furnish the artwork. John has come up with some wonderful, little-known oddities from Colorado's history. Of the 51 stories he has found, I was aware of only a few.

All of John's stories are just great, and it was pleasurable to let my imagination wander so I could illustrate them for you. What a joy to visually bring these stories to life. One in particular was very enjoyable—*"Hellhole on the Arkansas"* (page 37) That's because when most people think of Colorado, they think of the mountains—but a lot went on out on the prairies east of those mountains, too. I especially liked to illustrate this one because I had to find a willing model!

Two other illustrations come to mind when I think of my work on this book—*"Missing Locomotive"* (page 57) was fun because I had to create the illustration as a night scene. And the story *"Hitler's Ranch—The Myth, Then the Truth"* (page 71) gave me the unusual opportunity to dress Hitler up as a cowboy!

I'm confident that by the time you are done reading this book, you will have your own favorites to talk about. So tighten your cinch. Pull your hat down tight and mount up partner, because you are about to take a wild ride down some side trails of Colorado history.

Enjoy!

Dale Crawford
January, 2005
Fort Collins, Colorado

Words From the Author
The Colorado You Never Knew Existed

Real-life stories are the best stories. *Strange But True, Colorado* is based on this principal, of which Lord Byron observed, "Tis strange—but true; for truth is always strange; stranger than fiction."

Ever since moving to my Rocky Mountain home in 1990, I have been quietly collecting the region's quirky facts and wacky trivia. This book attempts a return to my formula used in *Black Hills Believables*, published by Falcon Press in 1983—keep each story short, readable, pair each with a compelling illustration—and when possible, build to a surprise or twist ending.

However, in *Strange But True, Colorado* I found it simply impossible to hold strictly to the earlier format. Impossible because of the richness of this region's past. Therefore, you will discover clusters of fun and curious facts in "Golden Nuggets of History." You'll also find a final bonus chapter, with the apropos title, "44 Tales Too Good to Leave Out."

As with the earlier book, I do not include a great many details. That's because *Strange But True* is intended as "history for non-historians," providing enjoyment even to those with only passing knowledge of Rocky Mountain history. Still, you'll enjoy the coming pages more with these few bullet points of Colorado history:

The First Americans

Long before Europeans arrived in present-day Colorado, people lived very successfully on our semi-arid plains and mountains. First were the Paleo-Indians. These included the resourceful Clovis and Folsom people. Hunters of wooly mammoths and other extinct beasts, they wandered Colorado more than 11,000 years ago—near the close of the last Ice Age. When European explorers arrived in earnest in the 1700s, they found the Arapaho, Cheyenne, Comanche and Pawnee roaming the plains, and the Utes entrenched in the mountains.

1706 – First European Explorers

Spanish explorers were the first white men to visit the Colorado region. They sought gold, found little or none, and left without establishing settlements. Spaniards did, however, settle in nearby Taos and Santa Fe, towns that eventually established satellite settlements in Colorado's southern San Luis Valley.

1803 & 1806 – France and Pike

The French also laid claim to portions of Colorado, established some trading posts, and eventually sold their land claims to the United States via the 1803 Louisiana Purchase. In 1806, U.S. army officer Zebulon Pike entered and explored the Colorado area. The first permanent American settlement was probably Bent's Old Fort, built on the Santa Fe Trail in 1833.

1858 - Gold!

Colorado remained mostly unsettled until 1858. That's when gold was discovered in Cherry Creek near present-day Denver. The result was the famous Gold Rush of 1859, when more than 100,000 people stampeded into the area in hopes of striking it rich.

1860s to 1879 – Hostilities!

Indians and whites fought mostly small but none-the-less significant clashes in the 1860s and 1870s, including the tragic Sand Creek Massacre, the Battle of Beecher Island, and finally the Meeker Massacre of 1879. Serious hostilities then ceased because almost all Indians were banished to out-of-state reservations.

1876 - Statehood

Colorado achieved statehood during America's 100th birthday, and has ever after been called the Centennial State.

1891 - The Second Rush

In this year, Robert Womack made the greatest gold strike of all at Cripple Creek, and a second Gold Rush ensued.

A great joy of this project was the opportunity to work with illustrator Dale Crawford. I knew immediately upon seeing Crawford's artful illustrations that the right words and the right artist had somehow found each other.

Crawford's style is compelling without being overly dramatic. And just like the stories, Dale's pen is occasionally whimsical yet always historically accurate. Note especially Crawford's portraits of historical figures—piercing eyes; and expressions so lifelike that we feel as though the personality is revealed.

Dale Crawford's evocative pen blended so well with the written word that he is not simply "the illustrator," but my full partner and "co-creator" of *Strange But True, Colorado*.

It would be folly to attempt to mention everyone who assisted us through freely given advice, inspiration or support. You know who you are. Your threads are woven into the fabric of this page and every page.

Still, I must specifically mention the lifelong creative inspiration of my mother, that daughter of pioneers Marian Berry Edwards. In 2003, at the age of 88, Edwards authored and published *Looking Back,* her prosaic portrait of homestead days in South Dakota's Badlands. Her efforts humbled me, and spurred me to completion of this book. But Marian's influence on this writer has much deeper roots, stretching back to the 1950s. That's when she began to show her children, by word and deed, that history is all around us. She helped me to connect past events with present geography. In this way of viewing the world, a butte or river or trail was draped in its historical context.

A few other souls I must mention— Tom, Cam, Mary, siblings who are, and always will be, the giants patrolling my mental and emotional landscape. And to Scott Ashbaugh, Steve Meyer, Ross Spalding, John Hughes and dear Lori Bonham, thank you for sharing the path with me.

If you enjoy this book, check out these authors for their fun writing style and sense of historical irony—Al Look (*Bits of Colorado History* 1977, *Sidelights of Colorado History* 1967), Kenneth Jessen (*Eccentric Colorado* 1985, *Bizarre Colorado* 1994), Abbott Fay (*I Never Knew That About Colorado* 1997, *More I Never Knew That About Colorado* 2000, *Beyond the Great Divide* 1999), and

Jerome Pohlen (*Oddball Colorado* 2002). Each of these capable authors provided inspiration to dig further into some known accounts, and to uncover heretofore unpublished true tales.

Dale Crawford joins me in hoping our words and drawings invite deeper appreciation of Rocky Mountain land- marks such as Pikes Peak, Leadville, Mount of the Holy Cross, San Luis Valley and the Arkansas River. Our work is done. It's in your hands.

John Hafnor
March 2005
Fort Collins, Colorado

Ice Age Coloradoans Camp Near Fort Collins

It may be the most significant archaeological dig in North America. The famous Lindenmeier Site, home to an inscrutable race of Paleo-Indians, is approximately 10 miles west of I-25 and a few miles south of the Wyoming border.

This ancient gathering place was discovered by amateur archaeologists in 1924, and then thoroughly researched by the Smithsonian Institution from 1934 through 1940. Uncovered were the many tools and discarded animal bones of Folsom Man, a hunter-gatherer who flourished 11,000 years ago near the end of the last Ice Age.

This culture's identifying icon, its great symbol, was the elegant Folsom point. This fluted projectile point is so intricate, so finely crafted, that modern stone tool makers using tools such as electric drills are virtually powerless to re-create it. How did Folsom Man make these spear points, and more importantly, why? The flutes or concave troughs, so difficult to execute without shattering the point, may have been crafted to allow more blood to flow when the point was thrust into a prey animal.

And Folsom Man's primary prey was formidable indeed — *Bison antiquus*, sometimes called the Super Bison or Ice Age Buffalo, was much bigger than our modern bison. A large male stood more than seven feet tall at the hump, weighed 3,500 pounds, and had massive horns that could stretch six feet from tip to tip. *Bison antiquus* became extinct not long after the Ice Age.

Another theory on the unique shape of the Folsom point says that it was lighter, and more aerodynamic, thus flying further when thrown. Then again, the flutes may have had religious significance. Whatever the reason, these magnificent projectile points were Folsom Man's crowning achievement. They rank him as arguably the premier stone tool artisan in North America, rivaling the best stone tool makers from Europe and Egypt. As if to prove that "technology" does not always advance from one epoch to the next, the stone-making skills of Folsom Man were eventually lost, and never again equaled in 10,000 years of subsequent New World aboriginal stone craftsmanship.

The discovery of several perfect Folsom points at Lindenmeier in 1935 gave rise to sensationalist headlines in the *Denver Post*: "Colorado's First Americans Revealed as Race of Supermen — Oldest Known Camp Site in Western Hemisphere." But how old was the Lindenmeier site? At that time no one knew for sure. The accepted date of first human habitation in North America was 4,000 years before the present. This date was staunchly defended by most archaeologists, including respected Smithsonian curator Ales Hrdlicka. A minority of scholars contended there were many archaeological sites, including Lindenmeier, which strongly suggested humans entered the Americas at a much earlier date.

Yet there was no conclusive proof of early habitation — none, that is, until the summer of 1935. That's when an extraordinary Colorado discovery would revolutionize the archaeological world. Lindenmeier excavator Loren Eisely uncovered a *Bison antiquus* skeleton (which could be reliably dated) with a Folsom point wedged between the vertebras! This was the equivalent of a "smoking gun," proof positive that humans occupied the New World before the extinction of *Bison antiquus* — at the close of the Ice Age, more than 10,000 years ago!

Mount Shavano's Mythic Angel

On Mount Shavano, melting snow creates a gigantic image of a female figure with outstretched arms...or are they wings? The "Angel of Shavano" appears and then disappears early each summer on the eastern slopes of 14,229-foot Mount Shavano. The image is visible from as far away as Salida.

Shavano was a sub-chief of the Uncompahgre Ute Indians. He was noted for loyal friendship toward white settlers. Kit Carson once convinced Shavano to help him quell an Indian uprising. Later, Shavano assisted in recovering white captives following the Meeker Massacre in 1879. Despite such displays of friendship, in 1881 Shavano and his followers were deported to Utah. At about this time, Chief Shavano's name was affixed to both the 14er, and to a booming miner's camp perched at the 11,000-foot level of this mountain. In the town site of Shavano, building lots were free for the asking with but one condition: you had to agree to grade the frontage of the lot so horse-drawn wagons could pass. One may still find a few boards and foundations as evidence of 300 souls who briefly inhabited this ghost town.

Several popular legends attempt to explain the mountain's "angel." One states that Chief Shavano had developed a strong friendship with the noted African-American frontiersman and scout Jim Beckworth. In 1853, Beckworth was severely injured in a riding accident. He would later die from the injuries. A distraught Chief Shavano is reputed to have come to the foot of his future namesake peak to pray for his friend. Legend says the snowy Angel of Shavano appeared for the first time the following summer, and every summer thereafter. This was interpreted as a sign that the chief's prayers had been answered— if not in this lifetime, then in the afterlife.

Another legend is of an Indian maiden who was moved to tears as she knelt at the foot of the mountain to pray for an end to a terrible drought. When the God of Plenty beckoned her to sacrifice her life as a condition of ending the drought, she complied. Ever after, the maiden reappears each summer in the form of the Angel of Shavano. Her tears, the melting snows, fall on the land below to make it plentiful.

In early years of Colorado settlement, many a pioneer credited the sudden sight of the Angel with providing enough inspiration to persevere through hard times. And whether or not one believes that "miracles" and "faith" could be inspired by a snow angel, the plain truth is that the "tears" or melting snows of the Angel of Shavano do indeed flow downhill to eventually sustain crops in the drought-prone Arkansas River valley.

Jim Beckworth

Chief Shavano

Our Nameless Peaks

The great mountains of Colorado sport colorful names. Among the famous 14ers, jagged El Diente is Spanish for "The Tooth." Mount Eolus is appropriately named for the Greek god of the Winds. While with the Hayden survey of 1875, a surveyor wrote of one peak west of Aspen, "Its snowfield in August, which is the month of least snow in the mountains, has an area of fully five square miles." That peak? Snowmass Mountain.

Colorado has so many high mountains that it has seemingly run out of names! Browse the complete list of Colorado mountains over 13,000 feet, and you'll notice that most don't even have names.

In Roach and Roach's nifty mountaineering book *Colorado's Thirteeners*, the authors exhaustively list all 637 peaks in Colorado above 13,000 feet.

Of these, 223 are unnamed, while 130 have names that aren't officially recognized. In one example, a mountain soars to 13,811 feet near Ouray, and Roach and Roach are reduced to referring to it as "Point 13,811."

With 353 of 637 high mountains *not* listed on the federal government's recognized Geographic Names Information System (GNIS), are there too many super big mountains—and not enough names? The rest of the metric world considers any mountain a "super mountain" that is 4,000 meters or higher. That equates to 13,123 feet. Every mountain of this elevation or higher in the Alps has a name. (By comparison, noted Japanese peak Mt. Fuji's elevation is 12,388 feet.)

According to federal law 80-242, *any* person in the United States may propose a name for a mountain. But don't try naming one after yourself, as a mountain may not be named for any person who hasn't been dead for at least five years. The person commemorated must have had "direct association" with the mountain, or have contributed to the area in which the mountain is located. A person's death while climbing the mountain doesn't normally meet the "direct association" criterion.

What's your best chance of getting a name approved by the U.S. Board of Geographic Names? Propose a name for a mountain that "…is not known to have a historical verbal or written name." Remember, there are thousands of such mountains in Colorado, and hundreds that are 13,000 feet or higher. The unnamed mountain doesn't have to be named after a person. Other imaginative names are encouraged. The board has shown a bias towards Native American names. It helps to get a local board or commission to endorse your name.

The government has a web site on this subject, a veritable cheat sheet on getting your name approved: http://geonames.usgs.gov/pppdgn.html#1-F. This web site even has a two-page PDF form to use in proposing a name for an unnamed feature. Send the form to:

Domestic Geographic Names
    Committee
U.S. Board on Geographic Names
c/o U.S. Geological Survey
523 National Center
Reston, VA 20192-0523

When trying your hand at officially naming a Colorado mountain, don't bother with one remote peak at the south end of the La Sal Range near Utah. It already has a wonderful if nearly unpronounceable name: Mount Tukuhnikivatz, which in the Ute language means, "Place where the sun shines the longest."

Early Travel — A Pain in the Butt!

Travelers could arrive at Colorado's Gold Rush of 1859 by neither waterway, nor railroad. Starting from Missouri, intrepid argonauts could choose only among the following difficult overland options (listed here from the slowest and least expensive to the fastest): #1 The bargain method was to walk, and push or pull belongings in a two-wheeled cart. #2 One could journey by a covered wagon pulled by ponderous oxen. #3 One could travel by a wagon pulled by mules or horses. And lastly, for those wealthy few who traveled light, the stagecoach was an option.

The oxen were slow indeed (plan on 30+ days from Missouri), but at $50 each they were cheaper than horses, could pull heavier loads, ate less, and were easier to care for than a horse or a mule. Stage travel was relatively smooth thanks to the suspension of the carriage from elaborate leather straps, but swaying could produce its own form of "seasickness." Mostly, stagecoach travel was fast, with the trip taking as few as six or seven days. This was possible because horses were urged to maintain a brisk trot. And every 10-20 miles, at a relay or "swing" station, six fresh, harnessed horses would be ready and waiting to replace the tiring team.

Western movies are essentially true in portraying the galloping arrival of the stagecoach in a frontier town. But horses can't maintain the high energy gallop for long distances. So galloping was mainly limited to arrivals and departures — a form of "showing off" or old-time advertising.

Occasionally a stagecoach was used to transport large amounts of gold. Of course, the specifics of just which stagecoach, and when, was a closely guarded secret. Such was the case when the old stage line between Leadville and Buena Vista was planning a large gold shipment. Lawmen had a hunch the shipment would be ambushed, so extra guards were assigned to ride along.

Sure enough, just outside of present-day Balltown, a robber jumped from behind a wall of rocks, and was promptly gunned down in a hail of bullets. What a shock when the robber's hood was removed, revealing that "he" was really a "she" — and even more incredulous, she was wife to one of the guards for the stage! In agony and shame, the guard couldn't bear the idea of bringing her body back to town. He buried his wife where she fell. Watch for the white gravestone, plainly visible from Highway 24 near Balltown. It reads "My Wife – Jane Kirkham – Died March 7, 1879 – Aged 38 years, 3 months, 7 days."

MY WIFE

JANE KIRKHAM
DIED
MARCH 7 1879
AGE
38 YEARS, 3 MOS
7 DAYS

Tales from Pike's Fabled Mountain

Pikes Peak or Bust! The very name Pikes Peak is enough to fire the imagination. Ask a cross-section of Americans to name a mountain, and 14,110-foot Pikes Peak will be named more than any other. Yet there are thirty loftier mountains in Colorado alone. Here are some reasons for our fixation on Pikes Peak:

One of the more curious chapters in the mountain's history began in 1873. That's when the U.S. Army established a post on top of Pikes Peak. But why, when all agreed there was no military value to a military installation so high? The answer was in a bill signed by President Ulysses S. Grant, directing military posts to collect and report weather conditions in hopes of forecasting storms, which often sank freighters on the Atlantic Coast shipping lanes. Because weather usually travels west to east, it was thought weather observations taken from such a high peak would be especially valuable.

The War Department paid $200 to construct a wagon road to the summit. Then came the telegraph line required to relay the storm warnings to the East. For this important undertaking, Western Union was paid $1,400 in construction costs. But maintaining a working telegraph line was extremely difficult in the high winds, snow, ice and hail of Pikes Peak. Even more problematic was the chronic poor health and low morale of soldiers assigned to the summit, where meager wood stoves provided the only warmth. During the short summer, lightning storms were a hazard. In such weather, the tips of fingers spread wide would produce bright, buzzing sparks. Likewise, a tongue stuck out during an electric storm might produce a blue aura of sparks surrounding a bearded face. Yet for two decades, the Army stubbornly maintained this highest of all military outposts.

Thanks to its dramatic location closest to the plains, for a time this high mountain lent its name to the entire Front Range region. Thus, gold-rushing 59ers bound for diggings west and north of Denver might paint "Pikes Peak or Bust" on the side of wagons. Years later, Katherine Lee Bates was so inspired by the view from Pikes Peak that she composed the lyrics to "America the Beautiful."

The modern mystique of Pikes Peak began in 1806. That's when explorers led by Zebulon Pike first saw the peak from 150 miles out on the plains. Pike later tried, but failed, to climb his namesake, estimating its height at 18,581 feet. He is said to have predicted that it never would be climbed. Ironically, Pikes Peak became the first summited "14er" in the United States in 1820.

It should be noted that Pike didn't presume to name the mountain after himself. He called it "Grand Peak," and it was subsequently mapped as "James Peak." But early trappers and military men refused to call this shining mount anything but Pikes Peak. So shall it ever be.

Colorado's Black Baron Stood Tall

When the founders of a gold rush hamlet below the Ten Mile Range wanted a U.S. Post Office, they cunningly named their new town after the sitting vice president of the United States, John C. Breckinridge. Sure enough, Breckinridge pulled a few strings to get "his" town a post office by January, 1860. Shortly thereafter, Breckinridge ran for president against Lincoln and Stephen Douglas on a pro-slavery platform, winning 11 Southern states but losing to Lincoln. Not long after, Breckinridge was appointed a major general, and then Secretary of War, for the Confederate States of America. That's when embarrassed citizens of Breckinridge quietly changed the spelling of the town's name to the present-day Breckenridge!

At about this time Breckenridge became home to Barney Ford, the extraordinary former runaway slave who would change the course of American history more than once. Ford was born into slavery in the South before escaping to Chicago, where he helped other fugitive slaves reach the freedom of Canada on the Underground Railroad. Arriving in Breckenridge, he staked a claim to what he hoped would be a rich gold mine on a little mountain southeast of town. Today it's called Barney Ford Hill, but Ford didn't own the claim for long. He knew blacks couldn't own property in a U.S. territory, owing to the Supreme Court's 1857 Dred Scott Case, so he retained a pair of white lawyers to hold the claim in their name on his behalf. That backfired when the lawyers decided to keep the claim for themselves. In an example of ironic and poetic justice, Barney Ford Hill turned out to be nearly worthless.

Barney Ford lost yet another claim to white claim-jumpers near Denver. But if gold eluded him, riches did not. Ford opened several businesses in Denver and Cheyenne, including two luxury hotels. By 1864, he was said to have the 14th highest income in Colorado Territory. One of his buildings, the three-story Barney Ford Building, still stands at 1514 Blake Street.

Because early versions of the Colorado Constitution denied citizenship and voting rights to African-Americans, Ford lobbied against statehood under such conditions. His efforts were a significant factor in delaying Colorado's entry into the Union by as much as 10 years. But this delay ensured that the eventual state constitution, adopted in 1876, would protect the right of "all males" to vote.

On one of many trips to Washington, Ford may have saved President Andrew Johnson from impeachment and removal from office. The year was 1868, and Colorado's territorial legislature had yet again denied the vote to all "non-Caucasians" in a proposed state constitution. Ford lobbied his friend, Massachusetts Senator Charles Sumner, who in turn persuaded President Johnson to veto statehood for Colorado. Had Colorado become a state, citizens Evans and Chaffee, who favored impeachment, would have become U.S. senators able to vote against the president.

Barney L. Ford, called by some the "Black Baron of Colorado" and by others the "President Maker," is immortalized in stained glass in the Colorado Capitol Building.

John C. Breckinridge

Barney "President Maker" Ford

1514 BLAKE ST.

A. Johnson

Living the *High* Life

Because Colorado is the highest state in the nation, with an average elevation of 6,800 feet, it's no surprise that many of the "highest" claims to fame for the nation and world are found right here. Can you name the highest county in the country? That would be San Juan County. Being the highest, it also claims to be the only county in the lower 48 states without a single acre of agricultural land. But wait! Hinsdale County is nearly as high. And with a growing season of just a few days, Hinsdale can also make the perverse claim of "zero" agricultural acreage.

What's the highest U.S. drive-to campground? Some sources say it's Molas Lake Campground above Silverton, though it now appears 12,010 foot elevation Kite Lake Campground above Fairplay is the winner.

But the real controversy is reserved for the highest town in the highest state. What is the highest town? Most guide books say Leadville is America's highest community. Not so says tiny Alma's Mayor Bob Ensign, 48, tireless defender of the town's only claim to fame.

"Those guys over in Leadville have always said they're the country's highest city, but there's never been any question that Alma is higher," says Ensign. "I guess the battle started in the early '90s, when someone down there—I like to say 'down there' when talking about Leadville—looked at a map and realized we had them beat. Their elevation was 10,152 feet (3,094 meters); ours was 10,355 (3,156 meters).

But Leadville is built on a slant, so they found a hill where they could get above us, and changed their elevation. It wasn't fair. They already had the site of Doc Holliday's last gunfight, and now they were trying to steal our rightful thunder. I decided we needed to rake some muck."

Continues Ensign, "Alma had just measured a bunch of elevations for a municipal water project, so we picked one in the middle—10,578 feet (3,224 meters)—and made it our official reading. We kept a few feet up our sleeve in case Leadville tried to cheat. I had our lawyer draw up the resolution: '10,578 feet (3,224 meters) and rising.' (These mountains are still growing at a measurable rate.) Leadville can be the highest city—we wouldn't be caught dead calling ourselves city folk—but it's *not* the highest municipality. That's Alma."

Leadville residents say they have just two seasons—ten months of winter, preceded by two months of "late fall." Such harsh weather contributed to the curious naming of Dead Man Claim near Leadville. It all started during a fierce winter in the late 1860s with the death of a prospector remembered only as Scotty. The grave diggers stuffed the body in a snow bank while they toiled through 10 feet of snow and six more feet of hard ground. After three days of digging, they inadvertently discovered gold. In all the excitement, Scotty's body was completely forgotten- until it reappeared during the spring thaw.

Scared of Heights?

Here are more Colorado curiosities relating to elevation: Colorado boasts of having had the highest railroad station in the country, possibly the world. That would be Waldorf, elevation 11,666 feet. A little later Corona Station, at about the same elevation on the line over Rollins Pass near Boulder, held the honor. Other high-point winners include the country's highest church steeple, and highest video store, both in Leadville.

The *Kokomo Summit County Times*, which began publication in 1880, ran its presses at 10,618 feet and made the claim it was "...published at the highest elevation of any paper in the world." Then there was the old-time magistrate in Animas Forks, elevation 11,200 feet, who is alleged to have quipped, "Persons have no appeal from a verdict rendered here. This is the highest court in the land!"

Living and working at high elevation is a Colorado tradition. During the Gold and Silver Rush eras in Colorado, many miners spent six months or more per year living in shacks near mountain tops between 13,000 and 14,100 feet in elevation.

[As the author researched lifestyle factors for Colorado miners living at high elevation, he came upon an unlikely source. Turns out that brother Tom Hafnor, with wife Jessie, lived and worked in the mid-1990s in the mining town of Potosi, Bolivia. The lower and upper ends of Potosi are 14,450 ft. and 14,600 ft. in elevation respectively—a bit higher than Colorado's highest peaks. What was it like to live and work so high? In such thin air, an otherwise athletic Tom and Jessie found they could not run even a few steps. Sleep was difficult, appetites suffered, and they had colds all the time during their half-year stay. At noon, the air might feel warm, but only in direct sunshine. The shade was always cold.]

The experience of South American miners residing in the high Andes have proven the limits of human habitation relative to elevation. It is reported that mortality rates spiral when humans attempt to live year-round at elevations of 18,000 feet and higher. Settlements as little as 500 feet lower are statistically much healthier.

Living at high elevation has its lighter moments, too—like the season when Leadville's high school basketball team learned that visiting teams were concerned about competing in the thin air of a gym perched at 10,152 feet. To make visiting players even more nervous, before each home game the Leadville student manager would conspicuously position an oxygen tank at the end of the Leadville bench!

ROLLINS PASS

Mountains of Sand

Colorado has some famous piles of sand. Best known are the Great Sand Dunes, located in the national monument of the same name in south-central Colorado. Here, billions of tiny grains of wind-blown sand have piled dunes to over 700 feet. Dunes on a smaller scale can be found in the northeast corner of Colorado's North Park.

But Colorado has other, less obvious sand dunes. They are part of the somewhat inaccurately named Nebraska Sand Hills. For you see, the Nebraska Sand Hills also spill into neighboring Colorado and parts of South Dakota and Kansas. And at more than 20,000 square miles, these hills amount to the biggest pile of sand in the world!

The Sand Hills are actually dunes, each covered by only a few inches of topsoil and a carpet of stabilizing grass. The Sand Hills invade Colorado in Yuma, Washington, Morgan and Logan counties (look for our Sand Hills just south of the South Platte River alongside Interstate 76).

The Sand Hills are sometimes called America's best managed cattle grasslands. It's true. If over-grazed, Sand Hills grass cover dies, resulting in "blowouts." In these hillside depressions, sand is exposed and relentlessly blown about by the wind.

But the Sand Hills weren't always considered acceptable cattle country. In 1796, Scotsman James McKay exaggerated somewhat in describing the Sand Hills as, "...a great desert of drifting sand, void of any trees, soil, water or animals of any kind." In the early days of the Open Range, cattlemen steadfastly avoided the Sand Hills, believing the grass to be inferior, and the water scarce.

Then, in the late 1870s, a blizzard swept through the Dakotas and scattered thousands of Longhorn cattle southward into the Sand Hills. These distressed animals were given up for lost or dead. But many months later, the missing Longhorns were discovered in the heart of the Sand Hills. Not only were they alive, but each had gained more weight than similar cattle outside the Sand Hills. Cattlemen took note, and quickly occupied the Sand Hills with herds as large as 50,000 head.

This ended the myth of poor grass and scarce water. In reality, the Sand Hills are peppered with thousands of lakes and marshes. This is because the sand acts as a huge sponge, collecting the infrequent moisture and creating a high water table and vast underground reservoirs.

And though few know it, this unique four-state region of grass-stabilized dunes contains more grains of sand than the entire Sahara Desert!

Long Lost Olympic Medal Reclaimed

For 50 years, no one knew the truth — America's first-ever Olympic medal in skiing was won by a Coloradoan, and in a most improbable fashion.

The strange story begins in Chamonix, France, site of the first Winter Olympics. The year is 1924. The U.S. team is captained by Coloradoan Anders Haugen. This native Norwegian had come to America nearly 20 years earlier. Haugen, 36, is personable, handsome, and so dedicated to representing his adopted country that he pays his own transportation costs to the Games!

Back in Colorado, Haugen was something of a local sensation for his ability to fly through the air on wooden skis. In 1919, he set a world-record distance jump of 213 feet at the Dillon ski jumping hill. In 1920, Haugen broke his own record by gliding 214 feet down the same hill. Dillon quickly became the epicenter of U.S. ski jumping. But alas, you can't hike to this world-record historic site, for today it is submerged under 200 feet of water, flooded in 1963 by Dillon Reservoir.

In those early years, Haugen could choose from a long list of operating ski jumps in Colorado. Places like Estes Park, Genesee, Idaho Springs, Allen's Park, Leadville, Breckenridge, Steamboat Springs, Homewood Park southwest of Littleton, and others. From World War I to World War II, Coloradoans didn't often ski, but they *did* travel great distances to watch others ski jump. In 1914, *Denver Post* founder Frederick Bonfils became intrigued with ski jumping, and sponsored a jumping exhibition in Denver. He instructed that a scaffold jump be built on Inspiration Point north of Lakeside Park. A reported 30,000 spectators came to view Denver's own demonstration of ski jumping.

Ski jumpers were becoming the sport superstars of that era. In 1924, Norway's citizens cheered when countrymen appeared to sweep all three ski jumping medals in the first Winter Olympics. The official results placed American Anders Haugen in fourth place. Haugen's best jump had actually been three feet better than the best effort of gold medalist Jakob Thams, but Haugen was marked down for his unorthodox style of leaning forward over his skis. (Ironically, Haugen's frowned-upon leaning style would one day become the favored style of all ski jumpers.)

Fifty years later, a Norwegian sports historian stumbled upon an apparent scoring error. To his amazement, the scores didn't add up! Upon further checking, the Norwegian Olympic Committee confirmed that the American was rightful owner of the bronze medal. A fair-minded Anne Marie Magnussen agreed that her deceased father's Olympic medal should be turned over to the 86-year-old Anders Haugen.

And so it was that in 1974, Haugen was invited to Oslo, Norway. Frail but beaming, he received his rightful bronze medal from Magnussen in an emotional ceremony. It was half a century late, but America finally knew the name of its first Olympic ski medalist. To this day, Coloradoan Anders Haugen's tardy bronze is the only ski jumping Olympic medal ever won by an American.

Hellhole on the Arkansas

What was the wildest and woolliest of all the Wild West towns? Perhaps it was Deadwood, or Dodge City, or Tombstone, but many would vote for Colorado's own Trail City. Today you can park your car on the shoulder of Highway 50 on the Colorado-Kansas border and walk south to the site of Trail City. There you will hear nothing but the wind, and see nothing — except for the crumbling foundation of a hotel. But in its heydays of 1885 and 1886, Trail City bristled with activity. Here is the story of the rapid rise and fall of Trail City:

Shortly after the Civil War, Texas ranchers discovered they could make a tidy profit by gathering the semi-wild Longhorn cattle on their ranches, and trailing them to Kansas railroad towns like Abilene and Dodge City — there to be shipped to Eastern markets. Sometimes the cattle were trailed further north to be fattened on lush Montana grasses.

But by the middle 1880s, the Great Plains was growing more settled and fenced, and these large cattle drives were increasingly impractical. To fore-stall the end of their industry, Texas cattlemen and contract drovers peti-tioned the U.S. House of Representatives to create a "National Cattle Trail" further to the west. This trail, a portion of which ran along the Colorado-Kansas border, was never approved by Congress. But it was in de facto use for several years.

Because of this proposed federal road for cattle, a new trail town was needed at a point where the trail crossed the Arkansas River and the Santa Fe Railroad. Some envisioned it as a sort of "Cowboy Capital." Thus was born rip-roaring Trail City in the summer of 1885.

Several factors combined to make Trail City especially notorious. Being a major stopover on the trail, this was a place were cowboys were paid in cash. The town was decidedly "wide open," with the nearest court of law a full 75 miles away in Las Aminas. Prostitutes were readily available. As special entertainment for visiting cowhands, the soiled doves of Trail City are reputed to have occasionally disrobed and mounted horses, to gallop naked from one end of Main Street to the other.

Saloons lined the east side of the street (author Al Look claimed there were 27). Each had a front door facing Colorado, but a back door that opened to Kansas! Thus, a fugitive from Colorado lawmen could simply exit the back door to Kansas, and freedom. Or vice versa. Other barroom shenanigans revolved around the fact that in those days Kansas was a "dry" state that banned alcohol. Thus, the empty booze bottles were often laughingly thrown out windows on the Kansas side.

Trail City earned its nickname "Hellhole on the Arkansas." But infamy was short-lived. A population of 500 in 1886 dwindled to a mere 50 by 1887, and Trail City faded away with the last of the great cattle drives.

Miners Made Colorful History

Americans stampeded to Colorado in both gold and silver rushes, making some mighty colorful history along the way.

Many miners worked in very inhospitable locations—some as extreme as Moose Mine, which was situated just below 14,000 feet near the top of Mt. Bross. In 1886, three miners were covered by the snows of an avalanche northeast of Gunnison. Despite being encased in snow in ominously named Deadman Gulch, two of the three managed to dig themselves out. By this time a rescue party had arrived, and someone noticed a hand sticking out of the snow. They dug in, and found the third miner, still alive, and seated on his standing dead horse.

In that same decade, Leadville's Harrison Avenue was paved with shining "silver." The prevailing imperfect method of removing precious metals from ore left a fair amount of silver remaining in the smelter slag. This slag was used to pave Harrison Avenue. In Victor, a nearby highway was surfaced with similar leftover material from the rich Portland mine. According to some mining experts, this highway would now assay at tens of thousands of dollars per mile.

Sometimes miners made mistakes, as when workers inadvertently started a fire in the Vulcan mine near Newcastle. The year was 1896, and that underground coal seam fire is still burning.

On the vast Uncompahgre Plateau, one mine yielded radium in the 1900s, vanadium in the 1920s and finally uranium in the 1950s, which was then the world's most sought-after mineral. In some cases, the same ore was put through the mill three times, paying off each time!

Miners in remote mining camps often had to come up with their own amusements. Horse racing and foot racing were popular, with considerable sums wagered on the outcome. To add incentive, a foot racer was occasionally allowed to run the race carrying the total dollars wagered on him. The winning runner would then receive a percentage of the winnings upon completion of the race.

In Grand Lake in 1883, the winner of one foot race had $4,000 hanging from his belt. When he dashed across the finish line, he just kept on sprinting right into the woods at the end of the street. Once in the woods, he jumped on a conveniently tethered race horse, and was never seen again!

Hot Springs Are Everywhere

The Rocky Mountain region is home to thousands of hot springs that bubble, dribble and sometimes roar to the surface. The temperature of the water, heated thousands of feet below the surface by Earth's own furnace, varies from a tepid 65 degrees to a scorching 181 degrees. Today's visitors to Colorado may come primarily for the skiing, hiking, mountain biking and scenery. But 100 years ago, tourists more often came to the mountains to "take the cure." In an era before antibiotics and modern medicine, they believed in the allegedly miraculous curing power of Colorado's natural hot springs.

Originally, Ute, Cheyenne and Arapaho Indians revered the steaming pools as sites of physical and spiritual regeneration. One of the biggest of the hot springs, sulfur-laden Pagosa Springs in south-central Colorado, roughly translates as "water that stinks." This didn't dissuade entrepreneur Albert Pfeiffer, an Indian agent and former scout of Kit Carson, from claiming that the departing Utes "gave" him the springs. He promptly developed the area's first hot springs resort.

Other resorts popped up in places like Steamboat Springs. In the 1820s, French trappers had heard the "chug chug" sound of the springs, and assumed they were hearing a steamboat — thus the name for this famous springs and town. Blasting for the railroad in 1908 silenced the chugging sound forever, but not the steady flow of warm waters.

The rich and famous trekked to Colorado to soak in the healthful hot springs, including Alexander Graham Bell, Rudyard Kipling, Billy the Kid and Susan B. Anthony. In Glenwood Springs, site of the world's largest natural hot springs pool, notable soakers included Buffalo Bill Cody, Doc Holliday, and Presidents Teddy Roosevelt and William Taft.

Hot springs attendance benefited from fascination with all things radioactive in the early part of the 20th century. At that time, science recognized that certain elements had unstable atomic structure. The rays emitted by uranium and radium were thought to be healthful, and capable of restoring vitality to "old" water.

One of the most popular quack products of the era was the Revigator, a large drinking-water jar lined with radium ore. As stated in a brochure for the Revigator, "The millions of tiny rays that are continuously given off by this ore penetrate the water and form this great HEALTH ELEMENT — RADIO-ACTIVITY."

Other improbable products included radium suppositories and the Lifestone Cigarette Holder, where already lethal tobacco smoke passed over a small radium source on its way to the user's lungs!

Today we know radium as the source of radon gas, a pesky and unhealthful gas that poses a problem for many Colorado homeowners.

Colorado's natural hot springs contain only small and mostly harmless amounts of radium and radioactivity in the water. But this didn't dissuade early promoters, such as those in Idaho Springs, who named a popular pool Radium Hot Springs. In Ouray, the local hot springs was advertised as "the most radioactive body of water in the world."

Plane Crash Sites Litter the Rockies

In the first century of manned flight, flying up and over Colorado's mighty Rockies has proven to be a sometimes dangerous undertaking.

More than one B-17 bomber crashed in Colorado during World War II. For example, a B-17 smashed into lofty Stormy Peak west of Fort Collins in 1943. To this day, the curious still hike from Pingree Park up, up, up to the crash site's twisted fuselage and scattered engines.

In 1951, Colorado's first major commercial airline disaster occurred when a United Airlines craft struck 8,861-foot Crystal Mountain, also west of Fort Collins. Fifty-five lives were lost, and no one survived. At the time, the Crystal Mountain crash ranked among the worst aviation disasters in U.S. history. Ironically, the plane's take off from San Francisco came only two hours after a United pilot's strike had finally been settled.

Four years later, in a more macabre disaster, a United plane exploded over Longmont, killing all 44 aboard. John G. Graham was convicted and executed for placing a suitcase filled with dynamite in the plane. Graham's mother, for whom he had purchased flight insurance, was on the ill-fated flight.

In the 1990s, two Rocky Mountain aviation tragedies are noteworthy: In 1996, 7-year-old Jessica Dubroff, her father and an instructor died in a crash near Cheyenne, Wyoming. Jessica was then near the halfway point in her quest to become the youngest person ever to fly a plane across America.

In 1997, there is the curious case of a fighter-bomber that for a time seemed to vanish into thin air above the Rockies. All seemed routine as Captain Craig Button began a training flight in southwest Arizona. But when he failed to return to base, Air Force officials became worried. After all, his A-10 Thunderbolt II (the famous "Warthog" tank killer of the first Gulf War) was carrying four 500-pound bombs!

In the first clue to the plane's location, residents of the posh ski resorts of Vail and Aspen reported a large military aircraft flying erratic zigzag patterns among the peaks.

For 10 long days, the location of the bomb-loaded plane was unknown. A massive search involved helicopters, U-2 spy planes and satellite imagery. People speculated that Button had committed suicide by flying his bomber into a high Colorado peak. But heavy snows and avalanche danger made it extremely risky to examine possible crash sites.

Modern technology narrowed the search to the vicinity of New York Mountain, or possibly Gold Dust Peak, located midway between Aspen and Vail in the Holy Cross Wilderness area. Finally, the crash site was located under snows on a sheer cliff below 13,365-foot Gold Dust Peak.

When snows melted, some of the armaments were recovered, as was the body of Captain Button. But it is military policy not to retrieve crashed aircraft. And so, the illusive "Warthog" bomber joins an estimated 28 other military aircraft still clinging to mountainsides throughout Colorado.

When you enter certain areas of the Holy Cross Wilderness, watch for federally erected signs warning hikers and climbers that their wilderness experience just might include an encounter with one of Captain Button's 500-pound bombs!

Colorado's Cannibal

Alferd Packer entered Colorado Territory dreaming of gold. He may even have fantasized of joining Zebulon Pike and Stephen Long in having a mountain named in his honor. As it turned out, Packer would live to realize a wholly unexpected notoriety as the only American ever tried and convicted for cannibalism.

It all started in 1873 near Salt Lake City, when Packer was one of 21 prospectors bound for the goldfields of Breckenridge. Near Montrose, the party was fed and sheltered by Chief Ouray's band of Ute Indians. Ouray strongly advised against a winter crossing of the mountains. Most heeded his advice. But a group of six, led by Packer, pushed on. Between Lake San Cristobal and Los Pinos Agency, they became snowbound. There was no way out. In time, they were starving to death.

Here the story gets murky, but it is certain that five of six men died in that prison of snow.

Packer walked out only when the springtime sun created a snow crust capable of supporting a man's weight. His story -- he became separated from the group, and somehow managed to struggle out of the mountains alone. But no one could understand how the here-to-fore penniless Packer now sported a fancy knife, a rifle they hadn't seen him with before, and plenty of spending money.

In an odd twist of fate, the five bodies were discovered by a vacationing illustrator for *Harper's Weekly*. His graphic sketches of partially eaten corpses were published by *Harper's*, which was then the nation's largest periodical. Readers from across the country were both horrified and fascinated by the story.

When confronted with evidence from the campsite, Packer admitted to living off the flesh of his companions. But he claimed to have killed only Wilson Bell, in what he said was a case of self defense.

Before a trail could begin, Packer escaped jail. He stayed one step ahead of the law for nine long years. Then in 1883, at Fort Fetterman, Wyoming, Packer was recognized by Frenchy Cabazon. Frenchy had been in the original party of 21. He remembered Packer's unusual voice and missing finger, and promptly notified authorities.

Packer was ultimately tried and convicted. Presiding Judge Melville Gerry allegedly made the following comments during sentencing: "Packer, ye man-eating son of a bitch, they was seven democrats in Hinsdale County and ye ate five of 'em, damn ye! I sentence ye to be hanged by the neck until dead, dead, dead!" Colorful, but probably not true, Gerry's statement has became part of Colorado folklore.

Packer avoided the gallows through a legal technicality, but was imprisoned at Canon City State Penitentiary. There "Cannibal" Packer become something of a tourist attraction, and made a tidy side income by selling handicraft such as watch "chains" made from his own shoulder-length hair.

After serving 15 years of a 40 year sentence, Packer learned that petitions were being circulated for his parole. Leading this movement was Harry Tammen, co-founder of the *Denver Post*. Governor Charles Thomas would need to sign the parole papers. But Thomas had his doubts, surmising that Tammen really wanted Packer as a side-show freak—for Tammen not only

owned *The Post*, but also a traveling circus!

On his last day in office, Governor Thomas freed Packer, but only on condition that he remain near Denver. In this way, Thomas denied any possible ambitions by Tammen and his touring circus.

So Al Packer gained infamy, then his freedom. He died quietly in 1907, and was buried in the Littleton Cemetery. His grave still attracts the curious. After the fashion of Pike and Long, he even has a 12,522 foot peak named after him. You'll find it just northeast of Lake City. But don't look on the map for "Packer's Peak," but rather Cannibal Plateau.

• • • • • • • • • • • • • • • • •

Golden Nuggets of History

The first known ski races in ski-crazy Colorado took place in the 1880s, and were of rather dubious origin. High above Telluride, miners of the Smugglers-Union and Tomboy mines understood that when the Saturday shift ended, "first to town" meant first pick of Telluride's reputed 150 prostitutes. In winter, the Swedes and Finns naturally found that the quickest way to town was on skis. So when the closing whistle blew, miners became ski racers...with first place getting first choice!

In a most peculiar historical event, Denver police and firemen once erected barricades around City Hall, intending to fight state militia and federal troops! This so-called "City Hall War" occurred in 1894, an era when city government was considered an extension of state rule. Governor Davis Waite had fired two Denver City councilmen, who promptly locked themselves inside City Hall. Most police and fire units were sympathetic to the councilmen, and took up arms against the governor's armies. Cannons were loaded, and firearms were at the ready. Thousands of Denverites flocked to the Old City Hall at 14th and Larimer to witness the anticipated battle. Most everyone expected Populist Governor Waite to order the attack. But he never did. Eventually both sides got bored and went home. The matter ended up in court, and thus ended Denver's "City Hall War."

Cripple Creek was a Johnny-come-lately to the parade of gold rush camps in Colorado. But it was one of the most rollicking. Myers Avenue offered every vice imaginable. Popular writer Julian Street wrote about this seedier side of Cripple Creek in an article published by the *Saturday Evening Post* (some sources say *Colliers*). Citizens became so indignant over the bad publicity that they promptly changed the name of notorious Myers Avenue to— you guessed it— Julian Street!

We call them the Spanish Peaks—solitary snow-capped titans rising southwest of Walsenburg that are visible 100 miles out on the plains. To Native Americans, they were the "Breasts of the Earth." There is a legend, unproven but persistent, that the Aztecs journeyed to Spanish Peaks to mine gold for their temples and pyramids.

In the late 1880s, one stubborn Denver farmer still ran his livestock in a pasture near the corner of Broadway and Colfax. Such real estate, even then, was a mighty expensive place to graze cattle. Denverites jokingly called it the "Million Dollar Pasture." Yesterday's cow pasture is today's Civic Center.

Boreas Pass links Breckenridge to South Park and eastern Colorado. In 1883, the pass represented the highest railroad crossing in the world. When P.T. Barnum's circus was scheduled to perform in Breckenridge, a train full of circus animals huffed and puffed up the Boreas Pass line, but couldn't quite make it to the top. The solution? Trainers removed the elephants from the train cars, and the great beasts significantly reduced the weight by walking over the pass. By some accounts, the elephants actually helped push the train up and over the high point. In any event, the circus train was soon over the pass and coasting downhill into Breckenridge. Some have likened Barnum's pachyderms crossing the Rockies to Hannibal's more famous elephant traverse of the Alps.

Ghost of Buckskin Joe

Fairplay stands near the northern end of a vast, treeless valley—South Park. Yes, South Park is the namesake of the irreverent TV cartoon. Fairplay was christened by gold prospectors who moved there in 1859, having been driven away from neighboring Tarryall by miners who intentionally staked more claims than they could work. "Fair Play" was so named because here, every man would be given a *fair* chance to stake a claim.

Back then, folks in Fairplay had another name for Tarryall—Grab-all. Those who still believe in poetic justice, take note: Fairplay remains a thriving town after 145 years, but Tarryall has long since vanished.

This area seems to have the most colorful names in the state. Take nearby Buckskin Joe. This boom town was started by Joe Higganbottom, who also discovered gold. And he did, indeed, like to wear buckskin. Legend has it that ol' Joe once aimed at a deer, missed when he tripped, and the errant shot kicked up just enough earth to reveal his rich gold vein.

But the town of Buckskin Joe is more famous for the story of Silverheels, a lovely young dancehall girl. Her real name is unknown, while her stage name refers to trademark silver-heeled shoes she wore during song-and-dance routines. Silverheels was a favorite of the enthralled miners.

When a terrible smallpox epidemic disfigured and killed a large percentage of Buckskin Joe's population, many townsfolk evacuated to avoid infection, and left the suffering to fend for themselves. But Silverheels stayed, bringing any comfort she could to stricken miners. She then mysteriously left town, some say because the pock-marking disease had robbed Silverheels of her beauty. Long after the smallpox epidemic, there were reports of a veiled woman visiting the Buckskin Joe cemetery. Some speculate this was Silverheels, returning to pay her respects.

This much we do know: Thankful miners of Buckskin Joe collected the small fortune of $4,000 as a "thank you" to Silverheels, but were never able to locate her or deliver the gift. Miners also voted to name the biggest and most beautiful mountain visible from Buckskin Joe in her honor. Sometimes called "the gentle giant" because it's so easy to climb, Mount Silverheels is almost 14,000 feet high.

You can see Mount Silverheels from much of South Park, dominating the landscape southeast of Hoosier Pass. To quote some sources, you may also be able to see the real Silverheels, or her ghost, by visiting the rustic Buckskin Joe cemetery near Alma. In *Mysteries & Miracles of Colorado* (Rhombus Publishing, 1993), author Jack Kutz gives this advice, "The most likely place to hear or see Silverheels is in the oldest part of the cemetery where the wrought iron and wooden grave enclosures stand."

First Railroad Across America — Or Was It?

12:45 p.m., May 10, 1869. History tells us this is the exact moment when a "Golden Spike" was struck to complete the first railroad across North America. The old photo of the Union Pacific and Central Pacific locomotives meeting at Promontory Point, Utah, is etched in our collective memory. But this is only part of a larger truth.

The event at Promontory Point was well promoted. That final spike was wired to a telegraph pole, announcing each ceremonial blow of the hammer to a waiting world, and triggering cannon blasts and celebrations from San Francisco to New York City.

This supposed first continuous ribbon of rail between the Atlantic and Pacific actually was interrupted by river cross-ings, most notably over the Missouri River at Omaha. Here the first transconti-nental trains had to be broken up into car lengths, with engine and cars ferried one by one across the wide Missouri.

Eight months after the Golden Spike ceremony, in January 1870, an ice bridge was completed over the frozen Missouri at Omaha. This continuous band of rails truly connected the oceans, but only temporarily! Within two months the spring thaw made the nearly one-third mile ice bridge too dangerous.

Thanks to the great iron bridge over the Missouri at Kansas City, the Kansas Pacific's plan to unite Kansas City and Denver by rail also promised to create the first legitimate and continuous trans-continental rail connection. (The Union Pacific wouldn't complete a Missouri River bridge at Omaha until 1872.)

Kansas Pacific crews worked west from Missouri and east from Denver. It was predicted that the Kansas Pacific rails would meet at Comanche Crossing, a lonely spot on the high Colorado prairie just east of Strasburg. Here Old Glory was run up a makeshift flagpole, and the two crews raced to be first to the flag.

And so at Comanche Crossing, track-layers met at the nearly forgotten time and date of 3 p.m., August 15, 1870, to forge a true transcontinental railroad. This was 14 months after Utah's "Golden Spike" event. In Colorado there was no golden spike, and little ceremony, though an estimated 1,000 people witnessed the meeting of the rails. Now Denver was linked to both oceans. Never again would the Mile High City see freight arriving by ox-trains, or passengers arriving by stage-coach.

In an interesting footnote of the rush to Promontory Point, elite tracklayers of the Central Pacific laid 10 miles and 56 feet of rail in a single day. This was a world track laying record. Union Pacific tracklayers wanted to challenge the record, but lacked a sufficient stockpile of rails. When the Kansas Pacific was nearing completion, some of these same disappointed Union Pacific workers transferred to Colorado for a second chance at the record. They joined other workers on that historic Ides of August to lay 10 miles plus 1,320 feet of rail to claim a new world record.

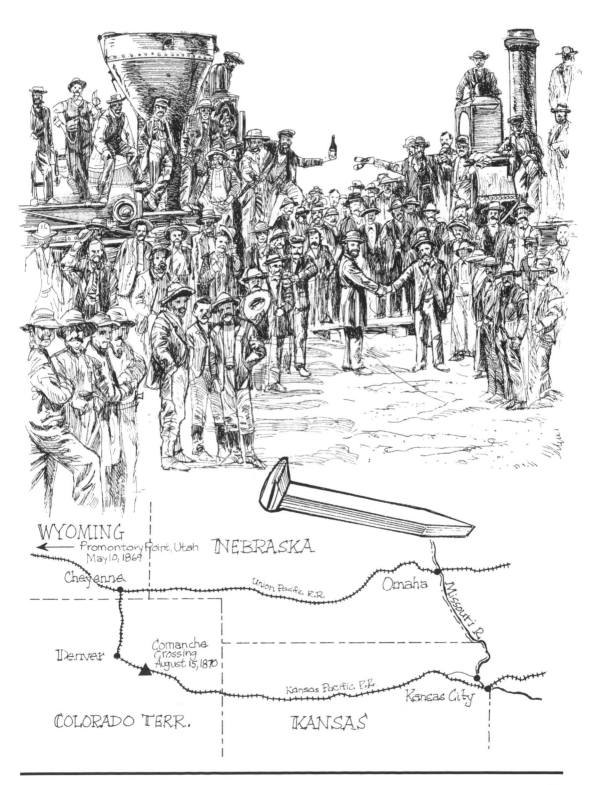

WYOMING
← Promontory Point, Utah
May 10, 1869
NEBRASKA
Cheyenne
Union Pacific R.R.
Omaha
Missouri R.
Denver
Comancha Crossing
August 15, 1870
Kansas Pacific R.R.
Kansas City
COLORADO TERR.
KANSAS

Kooky Colorado

Call it trivia. Call it weird facts. Colorado has more than its share. For example, check out the strange story of a headless chicken:

In 1945, Fruita, Colorado's Lloyd Olsen selected a rooster named Mike for the chopping block. Mindful of his mother-in-law's fondness for chicken neck, Lloyd aimed high with the ax, severing the head but preserving the entire neck. In typical chicken fashion, Mike promptly ran around like, well...like a chicken with its head cut off. But in this case, the chicken refused to die. Apparently, a tiny bit of Rooster Mike's brain stem had survived the ax—just enough for his vital organs to function. By feeding grain and water directly into the gullet with an eye dropper, Olsen was able to keep Mike the headless chicken alive for an amazing 18 months! Mike was even featured in *LIFE Magazine*. In a no-brainer, Fruita town promoters capitalize on Mike's unearthly survival with an annual festival.

As Interstate 70 crosses Colorado, it goes through Eisenhower Tunnel, the highest long tunnel for autos in the world. Further west, the Glenwood Canyon stretch of I-70 was the most expensive and most difficult construction project of the U.S. Interstate Highway system. After 22 years of construction which finally ended in 1992, the beautiful viaducts of the Interstate now transport cars 80-90 feet in the air.

In the Indian Peaks Wilderness south of Rocky Mountain National Park stands an 11,940-foot peak that is rarely seen, seldom climbed, and though 2,500 feet shorter than the state's highest mountain, has been called Colorado's most spectacular summit for its sheer knife-like thrust into the heavens. This stunning mountain originally was named Lindbergh Peak to honor the first trans-Atlantic airplane flight by Charles Lindbergh. But circumstances necessitated a renaming. It seems that Lindbergh had received a medal from Hitler, and later became spokesperson for the America First Committee, a group that sought to keep the United States from joining the offensive against Germany in World War II. At this time, Lindbergh Peak was renamed Lone Eagle Peak. While retaining obvious reference to Lindbergh's nickname, the new moniker was considered less of an endorsement of Lindbergh's unpopular politics.

Before whites arrived, the Indians of Colorado were familiar with a rock that would burn. This was not coal, but an ordinary-looking rock common to the Parachute and Rifle areas near the Colorado River. Some early settlers innocently built cabins and fireplaces partly from this rock, only to see the stones ooze a black substance and catch fire when the fireplace was lit. On at least two occasions, the cabins burned to the ground. The rock in question is oil shale. Oil companies like Exxon would eventually extract vast amounts of oil from this rock. By the early 1980s, 21,000 people in Colorado found employment in the oil shale industry.

In Fairplay, "Jack Ass" Is No Insult!

Only a few towns have designated mascots. Most are majestic eagles, roaring lions or other impressive beasts. In Fairplay, the unofficial mascot is the jack ass—otherwise known as a male ass, or donkey. But in the American West, the donkey is more often called a burro.

Fairplay's love affair with the burro came naturally enough. After all, sturdy little burros were perfect for working the many mines around Fairplay and Alma. In 1879, Rupert Sherwood was looking to buy a pack burro, because he had decided to go into the prospecting business. Word came of a miner who was retiring, and his strong 12-year-old burro was for sale. Asking price? Ten bucks. "What's his name?" Rupert asked, as he considered the shaggy critter. "Prunes," was the answer, which seemed somehow appropriate.

Rupert and Prunes soon formed an uncommon man-animal partnership. They worked hard together. Prunes even proved trustworthy enough to run errands alone. He could find his way down the trail and into town, with a note protruding from his empty pack bags. The general store owner would find Prunes on the street, slip him a treat, and fill the order based on the handwritten note. Then with bags bulging, Prunes would head back to the high camp of his owner.

If the birth and death dates of 1867 and 1930, respectively, are to be believed, Prunes grew very old. At 63,

he would have been one of the oldest donkeys on record. This much is sure— Rupert and Prunes grew old together. When winters in Fairplay's 10,000-foot elevation became too cold for Rupert's liking, he decided to spend future winter months in Denver.

But what would become of Prunes? The problem took care of itself. Prunes was so beloved by Fairplay residents that he could panhandle for free handouts at nearly every door.

When the end finally came for ol' Prunes, he was buried on Front Street, in the heart of Fairplay. Over his grave, citizens of Fairplay erected a monument of stone and concrete, complete with a bronze plaque. It stands on Front Street to this day.

Rupert Sherwood died the next year, age 81. In keeping with his wishes, Rupe's ashes were buried beside his friend of over fifty years: Prunes.

The people of modern Fairplay aren't likely to ever forget Prunes. Each year they celebrate "Burro Days" on the last full weekend in July. Centerpiece of the celebration is the World Championship Pack Burro Race, a high altitude endurance run featuring numerous teams of one human connected by a rope to one burro, complete with a loaded pack. Teams must race up and over 13,186-foot Mosquito Pass. The winner is the first team to reach Leadville! Promotional bumper stickers provide a nice summary of the race: "Get Your Ass Over the Pass."

MOSQUITO PASS

Missing Locomotive

The tracks just east of Strasburg, Colorado witnessed the true spanning of the continent by rail, as you read about elsewhere in this book. Eight years later, on nearly the same stretch of tracks, history came calling again. The year was 1878. A flash flood had collapsed the trestle over swollen Kiowa Creek, west of Strasburg. On that dark, torrential night, a Kansas Pacific freight train hurtled unawares off the trestle and into the creek's roiling waters. Those on board — the engineer and two assistants — lost their lives.

When morning came, the bodies were recovered, the damage assessed, and all the train cars identified and eventually salvaged — all, that is, except the massive locomotive! Inexplicably, the great steam locomotive was missing.

How does 45 tons of steel simply disappear? Could it have been covered up by the debris of the flood? In time, this would become an enduring enigma of the American West. Precisely 100 years later, in 1978, best-selling author Clive Cussler happened upon an article featuring the missing locomotive. Cussler's subsequent research into this mystery inspired his best-selling novel *Night Probe*.

A highly inquisitive Cussler conducted personal searches of the train crash site in 1981 and 1982. Then in 1989, he helped organize a massive search involving more than 300 people — from the expert to the simply curious. Teams of volunteers used metal detectors, magnetometers, radar ground-penetrating units and a backhoe. They found only a few fragments of iron, but no heavy mass of metal. Following this big search, the "missing locomotive puzzle" became even more puzzling.

Although this Colorado mystery never has been conclusively solved, Cussler now believes that research by Denver's Lloyd Glaiser holds the probable answer. Glaiser uncovered sketchy 19th-century documents suggesting that a locomotive had been excavated in the dead of night, towed to Kansas City, and then rebuilt and renumbered. Was this our missing locomotive? If so, why did the Kansas Pacific Railroad deny it? Cussler believes the documents point to a frontier insurance scam!

Buffalo Bill's Strange Life and Death

Just like Wild Bill Hickok and others, William "Buffalo Bill" Cody could trace his early fame to a dime novelist. In 1869, a small book by Ned Buntline chronicled and enlarged upon the real life exploits of Buffalo Bill.

But Cody, a renowned Civil War veteran, Pony Express rider, army scout, Indian fighter, and prolific buffalo hunter, would ironically gain his greatest fame as a showman. His Wild West Show brought the spectacle of the American West to Eastern cities, and played to adoring crowds throughout Europe. Stars included Annie Oakley and Sitting Bull. When parting ways after the European tour, Cody presented Sitting Bull with the gift of a gray horse that could perform tricks.

Thus began Cody's role in one of history's bizarre footnotes: In 1890, the Ghost Dance craze was sweeping Sioux reservations on the Upper Missouri. Authorities felt that old Sitting Bull might encourage the young "hostiles." As a precaution, he was to be arrested. Hungry for headlines, Buffalo Bill arrived on the scene to help bring in his old friend.

However, it was determined that Indian police could better secure Sitting Bull's peaceful arrest. On the morning of his arrest, the chief's trained gift horse was brought out as transportation to jail. At the last minute, Sitting Bull's followers resisted. The old warrior and several others lost their lives in a confusing hail of bullets. To amazed onlookers, the trained gray horse responded to gunfire as though it were back in the Wild West Show, launching into a series of tricks! Sioux on both sides interpreted the scene as Sitting Bull's soul jumping from his fallen body into that of his "possessed" horse. This tragedy sparked a series of events leading directly to the Wounded Knee Massacre.

After 1890, the Wild West Show was losing money. Cody was a superb showman, but not always the best busi-nessman. He made hundreds of thousands of dollars, but lost equal sums through mismanagement and question-able investments, such as the establish-ment of his namesake town: Cody, Wyoming.

A staggering debt to Harry Tammen, co-owner of the *Denver Post*, forced Cody to become an employee of Tammen's ragtag version of the original show. The new show continued downhill, until one day Cody allegedly threatened to shoot Tammen if the debt wasn't forgiven. True or not, Tammen is said to have forgiven the entire debt.

Cody returned to headline his own show, but by then his health was steadily declining. A doctor recommended the healthful air and soothing waters of a Denver sanitarium, near the home of Cody's sister. While in Denver, Buffalo Bill died.

And here's where a strange life became stranger still in death. Cody left clear instructions that internment was to be in Cody, the town of his own creation. When it was announced there wasn't enough money to ship the body out of state, controversy erupted over where the great frontiersman should be buried. The loudest voice in the controversy belonged to Tammen, Cody's old nemesis. Tammen maintained that Cody should be buried on top of nearby Lookout Mountain—not in faraway Cody, Wyoming.

The funeral was a colossal event. Cody's body lay in state in the rotunda of the Colorado Capitol building. State troopers were assigned to stand watch over the casket—not so much to honor Cody as to thwart an alleged plot by Cody citizens to abduct the body.

For nearly five months, the debate raged while the body was kept on ice. In the end, Buffalo Bill Cody was laid to rest against his final wishes—on top of Colorado's Lookout Mountain.

BUFFALO BILL

Boulder Ticks to World's Best Clock

The next time you drive north of Fort Collins on I-25, look to the west between Fort Collins and Wellington, and there you'll see a cluster of eight 400-foot-tall radio towers near Highway 1. These are the towers of government-run radio station WWVB.

But don't try to tune your car radio to the music of this highly specialized station, because WWVB broadcasts only one thing—the synchronized signals of the time of day. This incredibly accurate time signal as provided by the atomic clock at Boulder's National Institute of Standards and Technology (NIST). This atomic clock is the mother of all clocks in the United States—an official standard that is precise to better than a billionth of a second. Put another way, if this clock runs for 10 billions years, in the end it will be off by less than one second.

Receivers around the Western Hemisphere (and by shortwave to points around the world) use signals from WWVB and sister station WWV to calibrate clocks where high accuracy is essential. Technicians in Fort Collins even received a thank you letter from a scientist at the South Pole, who said he was "… receiving your signal great."

Other users of this free service include the military, navigators, and GPS manufacturers. In addition, astronomers use the super accurate clock to time the millisecond it takes an asteroid to pass in front of a star. With that information, an astronomer can calculate the diameter of the asteroid. In Southern California, traffic lights are synchronized using signals from WWVB. New York's subways run on time (usually) thanks to WWVB's never-ending signals.

Fort Collins' amazing towers also broadcast signals to cars, wrist watches and home weather stations, each having been designed to receive NIST signals. For owners of these modern products, one need never set a clock again. The station adjusts for daylight savings, leap year, and the somewhat obscure "leap second." This leap second must be accounted for every 18 months or so, because the atomic clock is actually more accurate than Earth's rotation.

One more thing—if you're curious about what the broadcast sounds like, try tuning in the station at between 1400 and 1410 on the AM dial. Depending on interference, you may be able to hear the "Coordinated Universal Time" given every minute on the minute. Or you can listen in on the same actual broadcast by calling 303-499-7111.

Bats and Dark Places at 9,000 feet

What do bats do when they need a new home—one that sleeps 250,000? The Mexican Freetailed Bat prefers to live in huge subterranean colonies. One of the world's largest roosts is in Carlsbad Cavern, New Mexico. How and why these nearly blind creatures occasionally seek out a new communal cave or mine shaft home is a mystery. In the summer of 1965, a group of Mexican Freetaileds moved into the long-abandoned Orient Mine, elevation 9,000 feet, on the western slope of the Sangre de Cristo Mountains. Since then, the Orient Mine colony has steadily grown to become Colorado's largest bat community. Estimates of the size of this bat colony range from 250,000 to half a million.

The Orient Mine bats always return to Colorado in the middle of June, after the long flight from their winter range in the subtropics. Neal Seitz, proprietor of the nearby Valley View Hot Springs, says "We know they have arrived from the south when we stop seeing mosquitoes."

On any summer evening, a strange sight repeats itself at the Orient Mine. Having slept all day, the bats awaken and relieve themselves. The strong odor of guano (bat feces) waifs from the mine entrance. This alerts humans that the bats are about to exit. At some unknown signal, these flying mammals pour out in a living stream that looks like smoke and sounds like a wind tunnel. From the high vantage point of Orient Mine, observers can see a river of bats winding in serpentine fashion down and across the San Luis Valley floor. All night they will dine on the many insects found in this agricultural valley, returning to Orient Mine before sunrise.

So vast are the numbers of these creatures that for many years their guano, a valuable fertilizer, was harvested commercially. The bats themselves are also harvested by opportunistic owls near the Orient Mine entrance.

Colorado has 18 different kinds of bats, and they are no strangers to high mountains. A few even roost above tree line at over 12,000 feet. But one thing makes the Orient Mine bat community unusual. While most colonies, such as the Carlsbad Cavern colony, are a mixed community of males, nursing females and juveniles, the hundreds of thousands of bats at Orient Mine are all males. Colorado's largest bat colony is for bachelors only!

Hidden Glaciers Crown Rockies

They are true glaciers, the southernmost in North America. Colorado's glaciers are remnants of larger glaciers that formed 4,000 years ago during the curious "Little Ice Age." The largest of the group, Arapaho Glacier, is also one of the farthest south.

Since the early days of the twentieth century, melt water from Arapaho Glacier has flowed from faucets in homes throughout Boulder. Hoping to preserve and protect its unique water source, Boulder city officials proposed buying the glacier from the federal government. In 1927, Congress surprisingly voted to accept Boulder's offer of $4,606 (or *$1.25* per acre) for the glacier and surrounding land.

Thus, Boulder became the only city in the United States to own a glacier. On a clear day, Boulder residents can gaze upon their glacier by looking west from the corner of 30th Street and Arapahoe.

Back in 1904, Boulder hired Fred Fair as city engineer. Fair's official job was to engineer water systems to tap high mountain streams and glaciers. But his passion became the glaciers themselves...and their potential to attract tourists.

Fair figured 99 percent of tourists would be unable or unwilling to hike to Arapaho Glacier. But he knew they'd drive there, if only a road was available. Fair proposed constructing a highway to Arapaho Glacier. He believed this road would be more spectacular than the just-improved Pike's Peak Road, or the proposed Mount Evans or Trail Ridge Roads.

Inspired by the prospects of such a road, city boosters began a major campaign to promote Boulder's glaciers. The advertising campaign appeared in 150 magazines and newspapers nationwide. There was one problem—the advertising seemed to imply a "hands-on" glacier experience. But without a completed glacier road, tourists faced a daunting hike or horseback ride to reach and touch a glacier.

Glacier promotion was led by the Denver & Interurban Railroad, which went so far as to rename itself the "Glacier Route." In 1923, this small railroad captured the nation's imagination by offering a $1,000 prize to any aviator who could land a plane on St. Vrain Glacier. This glacier, south of Longs Peak, offered the most gradual slope for landing a plane. But it was still clearly a dangerous publicity stunt, which initially attracted only one daring applicant: Barnstorming Bert Cole.

Cole was Colorado's best-known daredevil pilot. He expressed real interest in the stunt, but only if the Denver & Interurban would insure his life for $25,000, and agree to somehow get his plane off the glacier! The railroad said no.

Fred Fair began to wonder if he'd ever find an aviator willing to attempt the stunt. Then, out of nowhere, word came of a mystery flyer who would take the challenge! Fair caught up with the aviator on a field near the Larimer and Boulder County line, where he was taking people up for short flights. His aircraft was a tattered Curtiss Jenny biplane. The young pilot is reputed to have said, "I don't care if I never get her (his plane) off the glacier. You can see it wouldn't be much of a loss."

Fair now faced a dilemma. If the stunt succeeded, it would make headlines everywhere. But if the rickety plane crashed, perhaps killing the pilot, then the negative publicity would be immense.

Fred Fair reluctantly turned down his willing aviator, a lanky young man named Charles Lindbergh.

Fair had no way of knowing that four years hence, Lindbergh would gain worldwide fame by completing a far bigger aerial first—flying solo across the Atlantic Ocean.

The Otherworldly Valley

If one defines an "alpine valley" as being above 7,000 feet, then Colorado's San Luis Valley surely is the world's largest alpine valley. A mammoth 122 miles by 74 miles, the valley feels more like a high desert, probably because with roughly 8 inches of annual precipitation, the valley *is* Colorado's only true desert. A desert, yes, but just below the surface is a vast aquifer, or underground lake. The aquifer makes irrigation possible, transforming San Luis Valley into a prime agricultural region. The incredibly high water table creates interesting contrasts — sparse desert plants sometimes just a few feet from standing water, and lush vegetation found close to the Great Sand Dunes.

This strange valley sports some of the coldest weather in Colorado, but watch out for the alligator farm near Mosca! Here the flow from a geothermal well allows gators to bask in waters that are a constant 87 degrees year round. East of Mosca, one has a great view of the Sangre de Cristo Range, Colorado's most imposing mountain wall. Early Spanish explorers noted the strange reddish hue that sometimes settles over these peaks at sunset, and therefore named the mountains "the Blood of Christ", or "Sangre de Cristo" in Spanish.

When the valley town of San Luis became the first permanent settlement in present-day Colorado (1851), its Mexican citizenry set aside a portion of the town, called a *Vega*, to be held in common by the townsfolk. At more than 600 acres, this land is still shared by the community, and is presently the largest public commons in the United States. Watch for it south of the town center, east of Highway 159.

The San Luis Valley may have the highest incident of UFO sightings per square mile in the United States. UFO aficionados call San Luis the favorite earthly landing strip for aliens. The Internet is loaded with reports of strange lights from this area, and author Christopher O'Brien managed to come up with 295 pages of text relating to local sightings in his book *The Mysterious Valley*. Area cattle farmer Judy Messoline decided to build a UFO Watch Tower on her land, 2.5 miles north of Hooper on Highway 12. She accepts donations, but there is no admission fee for the scores of visitors who climb the tower on a busy day. Most hope to spot a UFO.

It may be mirages; it may be phenomenon caused by wind patterns. Whatever "it" is, people in the San Luis Valley have a history of seeing "things." This may explain why the area has long been a draw for mystics and Indian shamans. The Hopi tribe believed that human thought originated in mountains overlooking the valley; adjacent Blanca Peak is one of the four holy mountains of Navajo legend; conspiracy theorists claim secret military bases are hidden in the ravines; and New Agers talk of San Luis vortexes that will lead them to new dimensions.

Add one more to the long history of strange sights in the Valley sky — the previously mentioned town of San Luis honors the 1853 Miracle of San Acacio. During that year, all of the men were out hunting when Ute Indians attacked. The seemingly doomed women and children kneeled in prayer to San Acacio, when for no apparent reason the charging Indians whirled their horses around and rode away. According to legend, the Indians later claimed they saw a whole Spanish army in the clouds.

Wacky Laws of Colorado

It hasn't always been easy to get life insurance in "wild and woolly" Colorado. As late as the 1870s, American life insurance companies routinely denied policies to persons traveling west of the 100th meridian, which includes all of present-day Colorado. Under special circumstances, "travel permits" were issued to the westward bound, usually with an extra premium. Even these special policies, however, didn't cover death as the result of hostile Indian attack, as the result of a duel, or death "...at the hands of justice." Thus, a lynched horse thief would find his life insurance payment nullified.

Men of the Cloth were sometimes granted exemptions: Reverend Charles Morton, for example, sought and obtained a special clause in his life insurance policy that gave him permission to "reside in Denver City, Colorado Territory." The year was 1871. Most insurance companies dropped their Colorado Territory restrictions when statehood was granted in 1876.

The cemetery in Fruita, Colorado was reserved by law for whites only. But look closely, and you'll find the gravestone of non-white Charlie Glass, buried there despite the ordinance. Glass was a hard-working, hard-drinking African-American cowhand and rodeo star. Glass gained notoriety for his loyal, but sometimes violent, defense of a cattle ranching family during the sheep vs. cattle "wars" of the Western Slope. That loyalty earned Glass his place in the family plot of an otherwise all-white cemetery.

A 1912 Denver City ordinance required each known prostitute to wear a yellow ribbon on her arm to denote her "profession." In response and protest, Denver's ladies of the evening also started wearing yellow dresses, yellow hose, and yellow shoes. The ordinance had inadvertently become free advertising, and Denver aldermen promptly rescinded it!

Like other states, Colorado has its share of silly laws that are rarely enforced, but remain on the books. Colorado law still offers a measly $2 bounty on the extremely rare and generally admired timber wolf. In Sterling and surrounding Logan County, it is illegal for a man to kiss a woman while she is asleep. In Pueblo, it is unlawful to allow a dandelion to grow within the city limits. One state law supposedly still on the books states that a pet cat, if loose, must have a tail light!

But sometimes logic prevails. For example, if you ever had the urge to rip the tag from a pillow or mattress, despite written warning of dire penalties, Colorado is the state for you. It became a perfectly legal activity when, after almost no debate, the Colorado legislature passed a law making it so. Governor Roy Romer formalized the law in the Capitol Building by gleefully tearing a label from a pillow. "I've been worrying about the mattress inspector jumping through the window for years!" he said.

Hitler's Ranch...The Myth, then the Truth

Some stories seem so good they just ought to be true! Consider the following, which has appeared in more than one book, and many periodicals:

Like so many Germanic persons of his generation, young Adolph Hitler was fascinated by America's Wild West. He grew up reading many "historical" novels about the West, some ironically written by Germans who hadn't even been to America. He and his classmates played "Cowboys and Indians," as many German children still do.

Hitler's Propaganda Minister Josef Goebbels predicted American Indians would revolt rather than fight Germany because the Nazi swastika was nearly identical to an Indian thunderbird symbol depicting good luck. (In truth, Native Americans enlisted to fight the Nazis in high numbers.)

After Hitler became Chancellor of Germany, his government purportedly confiscated a mortgage note on a ranch near Kit Carson, Colorado. The region is a lonely Western landscape, peppered with tiny hamlets like Arapahoe, Wild Horse and Cheyenne Wells.

As the story goes, Hitler saw a chance to own a piece of that mythical West: He ordered the ranch property to be put in his name, then demanded payment of the note. The American co-owner of the mortgage, a Mr. Bower, refused Hitler's request, and supposedly relinquished a portion of the ranch to the German government and Hitler. For years this myth has continued — as evidenced by people who continue to ask to search the faded abstracts of little Cheyenne County Abstract Company, so as to actually see the name of that notorious dictator as a Colorado land owner. But the manager of the abstracts, David Larsen, begs to differ. Yes, the land in question was owned by German nationals at one time, but Larsen will be happy to show you all the abstracts of title for the land in question, beginning in 1907. You will search in vain for the name Adolph Hitler!

Some have conjectured that one Gabriel Eberwein, who lived in Germany but quietly bought the land in question in 1940, may have done so on Hitler's behalf. But there is not a single piece of evidence to confirm this. So how does such a myth begin? It seems to have started in 1976, when Doubleday published this mistruth in the best-selling book *The People's Almanac*. Subsequently, the popular German magazine *Bundt* published an article that hinted at a Colorado connection. "Did the Fuhrer want to retire there?" asked the article's headline.

So how long will the myth of Colorado's "Hitler Land" continue? A good myth dies a very slow death, as evidenced by the fact that the Cheyenne Wells Chamber of Commerce, the local library, the newspaper and the abstract office all still receive occasional inquires from authors and researchers. "We doubt that Hitler, even in his wildest dreams, heard of Cheyenne County's short-grass country," says David Larson. "But we still keep getting questions."

Frozen Dead Guy of Nederland

To understand Nederland, one must first understand what is sometimes called "The People's Republic of Boulder." In the 1960s and 1970s, when elements of Boulder's counterculture wanted to get "higher," they would literally go...well, higher—up Boulder Canyon to Nederland, elevation 8,200 feet. These free spirits proceeded to invent things like the world's only hippie rodeo. By most standards, Nederland was and still is an amusingly strange place. "Nederland is near a major ghost-portal between here and the afterlife," according to well-known psychic Amy Bayless, who was also Nederland's controversial police commissioner. "A lot of ghosts pass through this town."

Late at night, some Nederland residents have claimed sightings of the ghost of old Bredo Morstoel. But what follows is better than a ghost story—it really happened! Grandpa Bredo Morstoel was born in Norway in 1900, and died there 89 years later. Upon his death, he was cryogenically frozen in hopes of reanimation in some distant time by future wonders of science. The body was shipped to Nederland's low-budget cryogenic "institute" run by Morstoel's grandson, Trygve Bauge. Grandpa's body was placed in a Tuff Shed, and kept frozen—well, sort of. The preferred method for preserving human flesh at ultra-cold temperatures is with expensive flasks of liquid nitrogen. Bauge opted to keep the body frozen at the somewhat warmer temperature of -109 Fahrenheit by using less-expensive dry ice.

In addition to running out of money, the dutiful grandson was running afoul of the law in the form of the U.S. Immigration Service. When Bauge was deported to Norway, his elderly mother faced the daunting task of regularly pouring dry ice over her father's frozen body. When the media began reporting on Bauge's messy deportation and abandonment of his mother, it wasn't long before the story line included the frozen body. Elected officials decided this was a bad situation, and that is how Nederland came to have one of the few laws on the books forbidding the keeping of corpses on private property. But because a law can't be passed making something currently legal retroactively illegal, Grandpa Bredo was "grandfathered" in as the only legal frozen corpse in Nederland—and there he remains to this day.

When Chamber of Commerce types were casting about for a way to promote the village, they struck upon the idea of Frozen Dead Guy Days. This zany festival comes to Nederland each March, complete with tours of the Tuff Shed mausoleum, coffin races, a parade, and a Frozen Dead Guy Ball on Saturday night. You can even buy a T-shirt adorned with Grandpa Morstoel's frozen smile.

The first Frozen Dead Guy Days were held in 2002. Almost a century earlier, a curious sign appeared on Ted Green's general store, on the road to Nederland in nearby Tungsten. Did the sign humorously foreshadow later events? It read as follows: "WE HAVE POP ON ICE, BUT WE DON'T KNOW WHERE MOM IS."

More "High" Times in Lofty Nederland

Unconventional little Nederland is famous for more than just its "Frozen Dead Guy." In the early 1970s, James Guercio of the band Chicago hosted many legendary acts in his Caribou Recording Studio between Nederland and the ghost town of Caribou.

Guercio wasn't happy with the fact that most of the world's great recording studios were in major metropolitan areas. Those places offered vices to distract musicians from great music making. He determined to build a first-class recording studio deep in the woods and 9,000 feet in the air. Elton John was one of many artists who would create some of their best music amidst the solitude of Caribou Ranch. A partial list of others who recorded there includes Billy Joel, Michael Jackson, Dan Fogelberg, The Eagles, U2, John Lennon, The Band, Rod Stewart, Chicago, The Beach Boys, America, Amy Grant, James Taylor, Joni Mitchell, Frank Zappa, Neil Young, Stephen Stills, The Nitty Gritty Dirt Band, and Blood, Sweat & Tears. Alas, the famous studio burned to the ground in the mid-1980s.

Musicians were attracted by Nederland's natural beauty, as well as the man-made beauty of a reservoir on the edge of town. The 180-foot-tall concrete dam and reservoir are part of a 100-year-old hydroelectric project that pioneered technology later copied throughout the world. When Central Colorado Power Company came looking for a suitable reservoir site, it wanted to buy old Hannah Barker's hay meadow. She wouldn't sell. The power company then filed condemnation proceedings. The judge decided in favor of Central Colorado Power. Hannah Barker received $23,000, but lost her beloved ranch. Though perhaps small consolation, to this day her name is affixed to Barker Dam and Reservoir.

The dam and downstream hydroelectric plant were completed in 1910. A major ceremony was planned, with Boulder Mayor Al Greenman flipping a switch to turn on the plant. But there was one small glitch: When the day arrived for the ceremony, the plant wasn't quite ready to produce power. Here's how the *Boulder Daily Camera* described the scene in a 1985 story: "In the background at the ceremony was another man with another switch. He kept an eye on Mayor Greenman and closed the second switch at the moment the mayor closed the ceremonial one. The power that came on that day actually was from the Shoshone hydro plant near Glenwood Springs!"

Stairway to the Stars

Of the nearly 700 miles of Continental Divide winding through Colorado, perhaps the most imposing portion is a 12-mile stretch between Loveland Pass and Landslide Mountain. This is the Divide at its highest, steepest, and most intimidating. In the Gold Rush era, this daunting rock wall separated Georgetown and the "civilized" world from the ramshackle riches of Montezuma and the Peru Creek mining district. There was money to be made if a transportation link could conquer the Great Divide. Enter eccentric "Commodore" Stephen Decatur, who had the daring idea to build a toll road that would zig and zag up and over 13,207-foot Argentine Pass. This is generally acknowledged as the highest pass road ever constructed in North America. (Author's note: Some sources claim a portion of Mosquito Pass Road is slightly higher.)

Laboring only with the primitive tools of the day, and often in outrageous weather conditions, workmen began hacking out Argentine Pass Road in 1869. It was completed two years later. When the road reached 11,666 feet in elevation, the town of Waldorf was established. Waldorf boasted the highest post office in the United States. Although Decatur had a sound business plan and a well-engineered road, he watched helplessly as his dream became a commercial failure. Before explaining why, consider a related story of the equally colorful Reverend Edward Wilcox:

Wilcox was a Methodist minister with an entrepreneurial streak. He first proposed and then helped finance a railroad from Silver Plume up to Waldorf, and then higher still. His Argentine Central Railroad was designed to make money by hauling both tourists and precious metals ore. This amazing railroad, dubbed the "Stairway to the Stars," huffed and puffed to just below the summit of Mount McClellan.

The railroad was completed in 1906. In that era, Mount McClellan was thought to be 14,007 feet high—in fact it is some 400 feet lower. Never the less, the Argentine Central was the highest traction railroad in the world, with the exception of the Peruvian Central where it crosses the Andes Mountains (cog railroads like the Pikes Peak Railroad go higher, but depend on geared cogs for vertical gain). Tourists of the Argentine Central were eager for the chance to throw snowballs in July. They boarded the train in Denver, where a roundtrip to the top of Mount McClellan cost $3.50. Because Wilcox was a devout Christian, the trains missed considerable tourist trade, as they weren't allowed to run on Sundays.

From the summit, passengers were told they could see one-sixth of Colorado and 106 named peaks, including nearby Grays and Torreys. In those years, summiting either Grays or Torreys Peak was a very fashionable thing to do. For this reason, a plan was hatched and a survey completed in hopes of extending the line along a ridge to the top of Grays Peak, at 14,270 feet the highest point on the Continental Divide. This portion of the line never was completed.

Eventually both the Argentine Central and the Argentine Pass Toll

Road went bankrupt, but for somewhat different reasons. A softening tourist trade, a short season, and huge snow-removal costs killed the railroad. The toll road, on the other hand, was doomed by its narrow, terrifying descent down the west side of the pass. The road was equally frightening for both man and beast, and always a test of nerves for horse-drawn ore wagons and top-heavy stagecoaches clinging to hairpin turns. To this day, one may four-wheel up the eastern side of the road to Argentine Pass, but the western side is permanently closed, because as one local exclaimed, "… it's just too darn scary!"

• • • • • • • • • • • • • • • • • •

More Golden Nuggets of History

In the 1800s many western mining camps had one street dedicated to houses of ill repute. In those days, the trend was to relocate "The Row" or "The Line" off the camp's main street, giving the town a more respectable appearance. In Silverton, it was the notorious Blair Street; Cripple Creek had its Myers Avenue (site of the first rendition of "There'll be a Hot Time in the Old Town Tonight"); in Telluride it was Pacific Avenue; and in Leadville, it was Chestnut Street. Not to be left out, Denver had its Holladay Street.

There's more to the above story. Holladay Street had originally been named for the respected founder of the Overland Stage Company, Ben Holladay. But when the street became home to many dens of prostitution, Holladay is reputed to have asked city officials to take his name off the street. That is how today we know this roadway by its alternate name- Market Street.

Colorado's Mesa Verde was declared a World Cultural Heritage Center by the United Nations. But ironically, it wasn't the center of activity for the Anasazi people. Like the spokes of a wheel, ancient roads emanate from nearby Chaco Canyon in New Mexico, confirming this desert municipality as the capital. Chaco Canyon holds many, many mysteries. Here is but one: We know that very large ponderosa pine logs were used in construction at Chaco Canyon. We also know that the nearest stand of pines was dozens of miles away from arid Chaco Canyon. So how did people without horses, or wheels, transport such huge logs such a great distance?

What is the second largest earthslide (after Mount St. Helens) in U.S. history? Watch for evidence the next time you're driving between Paonia and Carbondale on Highway 133 (about 21 miles northeast of Paonia). It happened in May of 1986, when rain-saturated soils triggered a slow-motion landslide of 140 million cubic yards of earth and rock. Moving one foot per hour, the McClure Pass Slide covered the old highway. The pavement you drive on today is more than forty feet above the original highway.

"Colorado" Charlie Utter, whose wagon train transported friend Wild Bill Hickok on the famed gunman's fatal trip to Deadwood, made a small name for himself right here in the Centennial State. It happened on Kelso Mountain, located east of Loveland Pass. That's where Utter was confronted with a curious problem: How does one get the enormous weight of three miles of coiled one-inch cable to the top of the mountain? His solution? Unroll the cable, and string it on the backs of 321 burros, stationed 40 feet apart. In this show of human ingenuity plus animal power, the burros started together and simply walked the cable up the mountainside!

Mysterious Crack Cave, near Springfield, Colorado, contains within its darkness ancient aboriginal carvings that are visible just twice a year, and for only a few minutes, when a sliver of sunlight from the fall and spring equinoxes illuminates the cave wall. "It blows your mind the first time you see it," says amateur archaeologist Erlin Trekell. Trekell has spent 15 years exploring the surrounding canyons of Comanche National Grasslands, and claims to have found drawings of a long ship with a dragon's head, inscriptions in several ancient languages, and a diagram and message about a stellar conjunction. He and others believe the writings are from Celtic wayfarers who journeyed to America before the time of Christ!

Marble is remote, but worth the drive. Sometimes called Colorado's prettiest ghost town, Marble is also the location of one of the world's largest and finest marble deposits. Heavily quarried beginning 100 years ago, the quarry site is presently inactive. But to walk among the pillars and blocks of cut marble reminds some visitors of being among Greek or Roman ruins. This beautiful marble was used to build the Lincoln Memorial, the Tomb of the Unknown Soldier and many other famous structures.

Civil War Marches West!

Shortly after Colorado Territory's 59er Gold Rush, Eastern states were plunged into our national nightmare of the Civil War. No wonder the rest of the country paid little attention to Colorado issues including Indian uprisings, and statehood.

But the Civil War did reach the Rocky Mountains. In 1862, a hastily organized army of Union volunteers from the Denver area marched to strategic Glorieta Pass on New Mexico's Santa Fe Trail to stop the northward advance of Texan units of the Confederate Army. These Texans were intent on capturing Colorado's gold and silver mines, and with this wealth they would finance a Confederate victory.

The Battle of Glorieta Pass, sometimes called the "Gettysburg of the West," was a closely contested conflict until the third day, when nearly all the Confederate supplies were destroyed in a raid by Colorado volunteers under John Chivington. This same John Chivington, hero of Glorieta Pass, later became the butcher of innocent Cheyenne Indians at the Sand Creek Massacre north of present day Lamar.

Civil War tensions remained high in Colorado, and in 1863 a group of miners in Canon City captured a man named Burr who was suspected of membership in a gang of Confederate sympathizers. He was to be lynched on the spot, and the rope was already around Burr's neck when the town mailman persuaded his captors to spare the man's life. When asked why he intervened, the mailman's response was simple: He had a letter for Burr.

Near Fort Collins (and in those days Fort Collins really was a fort), captured Confederate soldiers performed such tasks as guarding the military haystacks. These erstwhile rebel soldiers were sometimes called "Galvanized Yankees."

Purchasing and protecting a hay supply was critical to a horse-mounted cavalry post such as Fort Collins. During these years a farmer showed up at the fort offering to sell a large haystack located a couple miles to the north. The post commander sent out a procurement officer to verify the existence of the haystack, and then paid the farmer in full for his hay. When subsequently trying to bring in the hay, Fort Collins soldiers learned their "haystack" was really just a large haystack-shaped boulder covered sparingly with hay. The military had been duped, and ever after this boulder would be known as "Haystack Rock." Today, Haystack Rock has become a sort of First Amendment billboard as well, painted with ever-changing statements, school slogans, marriage proposals, graffiti and more. Haystack Rock is easily recognized close by Highway 287, just a few miles north of Laporte.

HAYSTACK ROCK

Land of Rare Lakes

The largest natural lake in Colorado isn't particularly large. Grand Lake, sometimes called the state's largest glacial lake, is a bit more than one mile square. It shimmers below the Never Summer Mountains just east of Rocky Mountain National Park. There are hundreds of man-made bodies of water in Colorado larger than Grand Lake. Of these, Blue Mesa Reservoir is the state's biggest.

Colorado's second largest natural lake, Lake San Cristobal, didn't even exist 700 years ago. That's when a massive earth flow, known as the Slumgullion Earth Flow, rumbled down a mountain and across the Gunnison River, thus impounding the waters of the lake. About 350 years later, a second earth flow started from the top of the mountain. Trees standing at irregular angles show that this earth flow is still moving today at the rate of up to 20 feet per year. You can see this phenomenon for yourself, as well as lovely Lake San Cristobal, by driving northwest from Creed toward Lake City on serpentine Highway 149.

These are Colorado's two largest real lakes, but size isn't everything. Some of the state's most beautiful and pristine lakes are tiny—hanging ponds fed by glaciers and permanent snow-fields, perched at elevations of 13,000 feet and even higher. Water in these high lakes can have an almost tropical aquamarine hue. Such alpine lakes may be frozen for up to ten months each year. Some have whimsical or forbidding names, such as Lost Man Lake near Aspen. The greatest concentration of alpine lakes in Colorado—200 of them—is on the high, level top of Grand Mesa. If Colorado lacks impressively huge visible lakes, it *can* claim part ownership of one of the world's great invisible "lakes." The Ogallala Aquifer, a vast underground zone of water mixed with gravel, covers parts of eight High Plains states, including over 20 percent of Colorado. The Ogallala Aquifer holds ancient waters under a staggering 174,000 square miles, and contains more than three *BILLION* acre feet of water (an acre foot is one acre of water to a depth of one foot.) Now somewhat depleted by heavy pumping for irrigation, Ogallala was once the largest body of fresh water in the world. Even today, the waters of the Ogallala Aquifer would more than fill Lake Ontario.

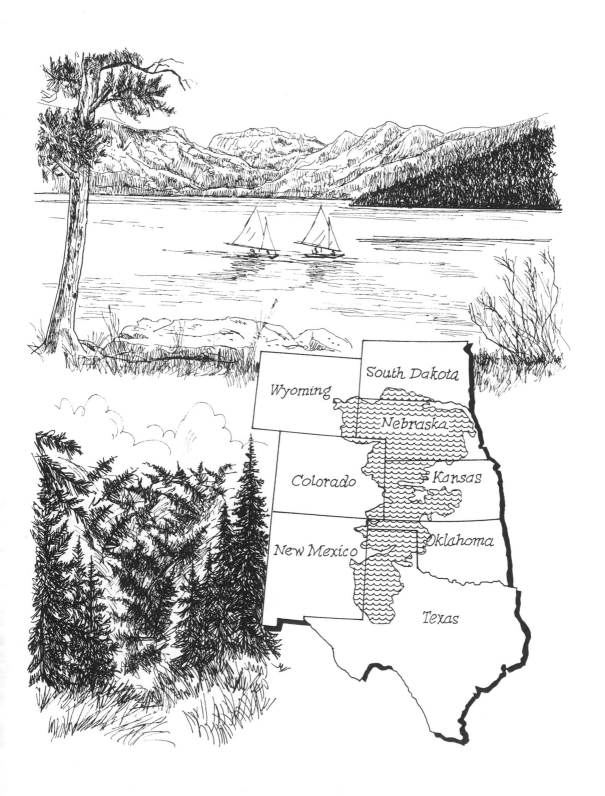

Electrical Wizard Shocks Highest State

Some called this Croatian-American the "mad scientist" for his creation of a "death beam." And it didn't help that one of his experiments plunged Colorado Springs into darkness. But in one tiny Colorado mining camp, Nikola Tesla matched wits with his famous rival, Thomas Edison—and won!

The seminal year was 1891; the place was Ames, Colorado (between Telluride and Silverton). For some time Edison had championed direct current electricity, or DC. Tesla, on the other hand, advocated alternating current, or AC, because he was concerned about DC's inability to transmit efficiently across long distance wires. The little Ames power plant was the first demonstration of AC power for commercial use. And thus, Tesla and Colorado pioneered electrification of the nation and the world.

Still, Edison stubbornly continued to promote DC over AC, which he considered a "death current." The only application for which Edison agreed to use AC was in New York State's first electric chair, as a way of demonstrating its unsafe nature.

Meanwhile, Tesla was busy with an amazing project. In 1899, he proposed to transmit electrical messages between Pikes Peak and Paris. He already had demonstrated that electrical energy could be transmitted through thin air—at a distance of 26 miles from his Colorado lab, Tesla transmitted enough energy through the air to light 200 incandescent lamps.

But Telsa's Pikes Peak to Paris plan required a still bigger experiment, for which he built an 80-foot tower east of Colorado Springs. From there he launched flames consisting of millions of volts of electricity—lightning bolts, really—that stretched 130 feet in length and lit up the night sky. Alas, the experiment also created a mammoth short circuit, which plunged all of Colorado Springs into a blackout.

Ever the pure scientist, Tesla sought little personal gain from his inventions. He did sell some patents to George Westinghouse, but retired to live on a modest pension from the Yugoslavian government.

Tesla died in 1943, but until the end his inventive mind was dreaming up new gadgets. Among these inventions was a workable "Death Beam," which he hoped would be used by the Yugoslavian government to repel Nazi invaders.

To this day, there are persistent rumors of the existence of a perpetual motion machine—the purported brainchild of a Stanford electrical engineer. But some say the machine is based on the work of that brilliant former resident of Colorado, Nikola Tesla.

Leadville's Radiant Ice Palace

For one magical winter, Leadville was home to the largest ice structure ever constructed in the Western Hemisphere, or possibly the world.

In 1895, the folks of Leadville were looking for a way to enliven their long, cold winter. After all, Colorado's "Cloud City" perches just below timberline at 10,151 feet, and can receive 10 feet of snow in some winters.

In those years, theme palaces were all the rage. Some cities built "corn" or "wheat" palaces, and both St. Paul and Montreal boasted "ice" palaces. "Ice" seemed the logical building material for arctic Leadville. But city boosters, tired of living in the shadow of larger rival Denver, insisted it must be the largest ice structure ever built.

Thus, Colorado's palace of ice would be gigantic—450 feet long (one and one half football fields!), covering 3.3 acres. The north towers would soar nearly 100 feet high, with ice walls five feet thick. But could little Leadville afford the $20,000 cost of such a grand crystal palace?

In late October, a fateful citizen's meeting would determine if support existed to proceed. Among the restless crowd were a handful of powerful mine owners. Doubters predicted the money would not be forthcoming. But at a critical moment, gold baron James J. Brown stood to pledge $500 to the ice colossus.

It was a turning point. One by one, other mine owners pledged similar amounts. James Brown may have thus saved the Ice Palace, but history chooses to remember him instead as husband to the Unsinkable Molly Brown!

With finances secured, construction began. An army of 250 men worked around the clock. Brawny four-horse teams hauled 5,000 tons of ice from high mountain lakes.

As construction neared completion, disaster struck. Leadville experienced a freakish December heat wave. Daytime highs soared into the 50s, and on December 12 the mercury peaked at an unheard of 65 degrees! The still unfinished Ice Palace began to melt away. Workmen saved the day by fire-hosing ice walls each evening to ensure refreezing during cool nighttime hours. Then typically colder weather returned.

For the New Year's Day grand opening, winter sunshine steamed through the translucent walls, filling the huge structure with an unworldly amber atmosphere. After sunset, colored lights embedded in the walls created a radiant effect. The interior offered a skating rink, a restaurant and a ballroom.

Organizers calculated the Crystal Palace would make money if open for three months. This would justify the Palace's rebuilding each year as an annual event. Optimism reigned when trainloads of celebrants arrived from Denver. But admissions soon dropped off. An early spring thaw sealed the palace's financial fate.

Ever after, Leadville residents have told tales about their fleeting ice palace, including this true one about products frozen within the walls as exhibits: A small brewery run by Adolph Coors sent several specialty beer bottles for the frozen wall exhibits. Coors sent an extra case of 24 bottles in the event of breakage. This extra brew turned up missing.

The missing case of beer was found two days later in a distant corner of the palace, but there was a mystery. Why had the thirsty culprits sampled only a few of the bottles? Expecting to find a premium batch of Coors beer, the thieves instead encountered a highly disagreeable taste. Adolph Coors had used salt water, colored to look like beer, to prevent the bottles from breaking when frozen in the walls!

Nearest Horse to Heaven

Could a horse survive winter alone on the Colorado tundra at 13,000 feet? With a little help, yes...as proven in February, 1956. That's when a private pilot flying from Denver to Gunnison was stunned to see a big bay horse stranded on the barren, windswept saddle connecting 14,420 foot Mount Harvard and 14,196 foot Mount Yale. Mammoth snowfields blocked any descent to milder climes, and it seemed clear the horse would perish without food. Gunnison pilots volunteered to drop hay bales from small planes. Such dangerous flights amidst the icy gales of the Continental Divide prompted volunteer pilot Gordon Warren to say, "That horse was getting the kind of flying out of us that money could not buy."

The *Denver Post* was the first newspaper to see the story's potential. Other papers followed, both in America and around the world. *Post* reporters figured they needed a name for the unnamed horse. They chose Elijah, after the Biblical personality kept alive in the desert when God sent ravens to drop morsels of food.

Commercial airline pilots flying from Denver to Los Angeles altered their routes slightly to give passengers a glimpse of the famous "Horse in the Sky." An Air Force veteran offered to parachute onto the Continental Divide to keep Elijah company until snows melted. *LIFE Magazine* declared Elijah ". . . the most worried-about horse in the United States."

From aerial photos, Bill and Al Turner of Buena Vista became convinced that mysterious Elijah was actually their escaped trail horse named Bugs. They flew over the ridge to confirm it was indeed their horse. In April, the Turners led an unsuccessful attempt to rescue Elijah/Bugs. Near the end of May, they tried again. Though snows were still deep, the Turners and others shoveled their way to the horse, leading him down through narrow pathways in the snowfields.

Overnight, Coloradoans who awakened each morning to ask, "How's Elijah?" were now suddenly asking to actually *see* Elijah. Accordingly, a parade was organized through downtown Denver. Centennial Race Track showcased Elijah in its winner circle, where officials draped the bewildered gelding with flowers and a colorful winner's blanket. A special stall was constructed in the lobby of the Brown Palace, and thus Elijah became one of the famed hotel's most unusual guests.

But Elijah was, after all, really just Bugs the mountain horse. And his handlers could see that this horse was increasingly unhappy in the big city. So festivities were cut short. Bugs was returned to his beloved alpine pastures, where he lived a long and uneventful life as a trail mount.

Bill Turner always maintained that this particular horse had an aversion to all things urban, especially automobiles and women in skirts — which is why, in the wintry weeks of the rescue attempts, a *Denver Post* columnist had raised a troubling possibility: "Perhaps this horse in the clouds does not wish to be rescued, but is exactly where he wants to be!"

Rocky Mountain Weird

Following the Sand Creek Massacre of 1864, and the loss of many innocent Indian lives southeast of present-day Kit Carson, the Cheyenne sought revenge by attacking Julesburg. They burned part of the town and much of the surrounding prairie, including telegraph poles leading into town. This effectively isolated Julesburg. The town telegraph operator, an ingenious fellow, devised a plan to send word of the town's plight to the outside world. He walked several miles to the nearest still-standing telegraph pole. There, he used an axe to tap out the dots and dashes of a Morse Code message. He was able to receive the return message, saying help was coming, only because he willingly put the ends of the wire in his mouth, thereby feeling and decoding the message as a series of short and long shocks to his tongue!

You can't spit to the bottom of Colorado's Black Canyon. In some places it is nearly 2,600 feet deep, pretty much straight down, and your spittle will evaporate long before it reaches the canyon floor. A scant 1,300 feet across at the top, the canyon features parking lots on both rims. But to drive your car from one parking lot to the other is a winding journey of roughly 65 miles and takes three or more hours! As of this writing, Black Canyon is the nation's newest National Park. And though this canyon rivals the Grand Canyon in splendor, there's a high likelihood you've never seen it, because the Black Canyon is still relatively unknown to American tourists.

Colorado's oldest tree was already more than 400 years old when Jesus walked the streets of Nazareth. Fearing vandalism, forestry experts won't reveal the exact location of this bristlecone pine, which recently "celebrated" birthday number 2,441. But we do know this Methuselah of a tree stands somewhere among ancient windgnarled trees in a reserve known as the Windy Ridge Bristlecones on Mount Bross, north of Alma.

Okay, you want to see some natural bridges. You'll probably follow the crowds to Utah's Natural Bridges National Monument or Arches National Park, right? Not so fast. Consider staying right here in Colorado for a more authentic sense of discovery as you trek some lonely canyon and come upon a great natural bridge. Little-known Rattlesnake Canyon, six miles west of Fruita, boasts the second largest group of natural stone arches in the United States. You'll enjoy these arches in relative solitude (you may be the only one there on weekdays), but it won't be easy. You should plan for a round-trip hike of four to five miles—minimum. Find detailed directions to Rattlesnake Canyon at www.blackrabbit.com/rcanyon.htm, or through the Bureau of Land Management.

When the KKK Ruled Kolorado

In 1924, the Ku Klux Klan infiltrated both major parties in Colorado, and succeeded in electing loyal Klan members as governor, and U.S. senator. Klansmen even controlled the State Assembly. We may think of the KKK as a Southern phenomenon, but Colorado and Indiana were home to the Klan's greatest political success.

How could it happen? Then as now, the Klan lured members by denigrating Americans who weren't Protestant, white and native born. With few local blacks and Jews to target, Colorado's Klan went after Catholics. Persecution of Catholics began in Colorado in the 1890s with the formation of militant anti-Catholic associations such as the Knights of Luther. These factions boycotted Catholic-owned businesses, and black-listed Catholic political candidates. They made it hard for Catholic job seekers, especially teachers, to find employment. Rumors were circulated of a Vatican conspiracy to take over the world! Some Colorado believers in this trumped up conspiracy routinely tore the fabled Papal mark off the corner of dollar bills.

When first elected Denver's mayor, Ben Stapleton, namesake of Stapleton Airport, downplayed his membership in the KKK. But in a recall election, Democrat Stapleton was somewhat more open about his affiliation, even addressing a large hooded gathering at an Invisible Empire compound on South Table Mountain. Stapleton eventually appointed many Klansmen to government posts, including Chief of Police Bill Candlish. Candlish would later enforce a forgotten Denver ordinance that prohibited "...Greek, Japanese, Chinese, Mexican and negro businessmen from employing white women".

The Klan enjoyed even greater success by using Republican Party machinery in the infamous elections of 1924. Gubernatorial candidate and Klan member Clarence Morley said, "Not for myself, mind you, do I wish to run, but for the benefit of the Klan." Under clear skies on November 4, voters went to the polls and gave the Ku Klux Klan control of Colorado. Morley became governor, and Klansman Rice Means became U.S. senator. Klan-supported candidates assumed the offices of lieutenant governor, secretary of state, attorney general and state supreme court justice. True to his campaign slogan, "Every Man under the Capitol Dome a Klansman," Morley tried to eliminate Catholics from government.

A week after the election, Imperial Wizard Hiram Evans and the Grand Dragons of several states arrived at Union Station to bask in the great victory. A motorcade flanked by Denver police officers brought the "dignitaries" through downtown to the Brown Palace for festivities. That night, 35,000 Coloradoans packed Cotton Mills Stadium in south Denver to hear the Imperial Wizard speak.

Back then, many businesses sported Klan stickers on the front door. Kool Kozy Kafe, at 15th and Curtis, was a notorious Klan-owned hangout. A sign in the window read, "We serve fish every day — except Friday!"

Perhaps it all started on a summer evening six months before the November election, when thousands of hooded men gathered on South Table Mountain to await results of Denver's mayoral election. When victory for their candidate was assured, several giant

Gov. Morley

crosses were set ablaze. These burning crosses could be seen from Denver...and suddenly the Invisible Empire was not so invisible.

Oh, but Colorado wasn't alone. Peek at this list of famous card-carrying members of the KKK: President Warren G. Harding, future president Harry S. Truman, Mt. Rushmore sculptor Gutzon Borglum, future Supreme Court Justice Hugo Black, and at least five U.S. senators, four governors and countless other public figures.

• • • • • • • • • • • • • • • • • •

Yet More Golden Nuggets of History

Paul Revere's ride seems like a small thing when compared with Joe Rankin's ride. Rankin was a scout for Army Major Thornburg, who was attempting to rescue survivors of the Meeker Massacre in the Ute uprising of 1879. However, Thornburg was killed and his troops ambushed and pinned down southwest of present-day Craig, Colorado by hostile Utes. That's when Rankin volunteered to go for help. He slipped through the Indian lines, and set out on his epic rescue ride to Fort Russell east of Rawlins, Wyoming — 165 rugged miles to the northeast. Rankin changed horses twice, but rode the entire distance without relief, arriving at Fort Russell in 28 hours!

Fossil records confirm that northwest Colorado was subtropical during the Eocene Period, 37 million to 58 million years ago — complete with palm trees, crocodiles and flamingoes. But when climatologist Lisa Sloan created computer models of this climate by factoring in carbon dioxide levels, ocean currents and other known data, her models always came up too cold — so cold in winter that water would have frozen, which would have killed the crocodiles! She was stumped, until incorporating two lakes in her complex computer model, each the size of Lake Erie. Those lakes really existed. And they retained enough summer heat to moderate winter temperatures by 15 degrees Fahrenheit. And *that* was enough to explain why the crocs and palm trees didn't freeze!

As detailed elsewhere in this book, the Ku Klux Klan briefly ruled Colorado by sweeping the 1924 elections. The result was control of the governorship, state legislature and other high offices. Two Klan-sponsored bills targeting Catholics were nearly successful; the first was legislation to require all students to attend public schools; the second anti-Catholic bill would have prohibited the use of wine in church sacraments. On the final vote, six Republican non-Klan senators joined Democrats to narrowly defeat the proposed laws.

There are ancient Indian legends of a sacred highway connecting sub-arctic Canada with the subtropics of Mexico. Yesterday's mythic Old North Trail is today's historical fact—a pathway many archaeologists believe was used for more than 10,000 years. The trail, actually a series of braided trails, took advantage of a warmer, moister foothills zone where the Rocky Mountains meet the plains. Bits and pieces of the trail through Alberta, Montana, Wyoming, Colorado and New Mexico are said to be detectable in aerial and satellite photography. Hugging the mountains near Fort Collins, Golden, Colorado Springs, Pueblo and Walsenburg, this trail was traveled first on foot, then with dogs pulling cargo-laden travois, and finally with horses. Peter Stark, writing in *Smithsonian* magazine, suggests the ice-free Old North Trail may have been a key avenue for Asians populating the New World.

We are able to judge the age and length of residency of Mesa Verde's cliff dwellings through the curious science of dendrochronology, which can date past events through tree ring growth. Simply put, climate creates a distinctive pattern of tree rings, thicker in wet years and thinner in dry years. By matching patterns in progressively older trees, scientists can determine with startling accuracy the construction year of a Mesa Verde dwelling by analyzing the tree rings of a rafter log.

Road Builders Scale Peaks

The Rocky Mountains, always a sightseer's dream, also have been a highway engineer's nightmare. Among these hard-to-build roads is America's highest paved road to the summit of Mount Evans. The road was financed by the City of Denver at the urging of Mayor Speer, who was jealous of tourist dollars going to Colorado Springs because of the road to the top of Pikes Peak.

The Pikes Peak and Cascade Toll Road, fit mostly for carriages, was completed in 1888. In 1901, the first automobile lumbered to the summit. It was a two-cylinder Locomobile Steamer. Pike's Peak road wouldn't be officially upgraded to accommodate automobiles until 1915, though it was never paved to the top.

It was in 1917 that Denver countered the Pikes Peak auto road by approving funds for the road up nearby Mount Evans, a taller though decidedly less famous 14er just west of the Mile High City. Construction, hampered by three seasons of brutal weather, wasn't completed until 1927.

At one time there was a grand plan to link several of Colorado's 14ers by automobile roads, including Longs Peak. But times have changed. People now prefer to zoom up their mountains on foot, and it appears unlikely that any more of Colorado's 54 14,000-foot peaks will join Pikes and Evans in having roads to the summit.

The first Pikes Peak Hill Climb race was held in 1916 to commemorate the opening of the Pikes Peak Highway. It is the second oldest auto race in the United States (the Indy 500 being the oldest). The 12.5 mile course includes more than 156 curves!

Mountaintop roads were meant to lure tourists, and came about only with the advent of the automobile. In prior years, the challenge was to build roads that connected valleys, not mountaintops. The first road over Loveland Pass, above the present Eisenhower Tunnel, was built in 1879. Called the Highline Wagon Road, it wasn't a tourist attraction but a business venture in the form of a toll road. The charge to cross the pass was $1 for a team and wagon, 30 cents for a horseman, and 10 cents each for cattle or donkeys. Sheep, hogs or goats crossed for just a nickel each. Like most pass roads, the Berthoud Pass Road was a toll road until bought by the state to become the first free crossing of the Continental Divide which separates Colorado's Eastern Slope and Western Slope.

Colorado has other high roads of note. Trail Ridge Road spans the Continental Divide in Rocky Mountain National Park. The highpoint is 12,183 feet above sea level, making it the highest paved through road (a road that actually goes somewhere) in the nation!

The nation's highest through road — paved or not? Take your pick. Some say it is Argentine Pass, but that road is currently blocked to all traffic west of the pass. So the probable winner is Mosquito Pass, which connects Fairplay and Leadville by negotiating a 13,186-foot "low point" in the Mosquito Range.

Lands End Road over Grand Mesa is an "also ran" to Black Bear Road high above Telluride, generally conceded to be Colorado's most extreme "white knuckle" road. Nobody knows for sure how the Million Dollar Highway between Silverton and Ouray got its name. Was it because of the sometimes scary million-dollar views, or was it based on the alleged value of the gold and silver ore-bearing fill that was used to construct the road?

Which brings us to the Oh My God Road north of Idaho Springs, clinging to sheer drop-offs above Virginia Canyon. Tourists have been known to brazenly drive up this road, only to seek out a local in Central City to drive them back down!

PIKES PEAK
HILL CLIMB

Those Crazy 14ers!

For almost 700 miles, the serpentine Continental Divide winds through Colorado. Ironically, only a few of the state's celebrated 14,000-foot peaks are on the Great Divide. Among those not on the Divide are the eight highest peaks, including Mount Lincoln.

When Abraham Lincoln learned his name had been placed on what was then thought to be Colorado's highest mountain, he was so impressed that he sent personal friend and future vice president of the United States Schuyler Colfax to thank the miners who had christened the mountain "Lincoln." (Colfax himself must have impressed Coloradoans, as subsequently Denver's Colfax Avenue was named in his honor.) Mount Lincoln's height was variously estimated at between 15,000 and 18,000 feet. Noted mining engineer Albert Dubois estimated its height at 17,500 feet. Lincolns' message of thanks to the miners is said to have been the last proclamation he composed before his assassination.

Alas, Mount Lincoln wasn't Colorado's highest peak, but rather in eighth place. However, Mount Lincoln and sister 14ers Democrat and Bross did have an abundance of silver. Small mines and prospect holes multiplied on these peaks in the years before the Great Silver Crash of 1893. Perhaps Colorado's highest large mine, the Moose Mine, operated year-round on the arctic northeast slope of Mount Bross, just below 14,000 feet! Old-time prospectors maintained that the best silver lodes were above timberline, and the higher the better. They often repeated this short poem:

A good silver mine
Is above timberline
Ten times out of nine.

Blanca Peak is the Colorado 14er with everything—a commanding position at the southern end of the Sangre de Cristo range, status as one of the four Holy Mountains of the Navajo nation, and a claim to the southernmost glacier in North America.

Blanca Peak even had its own "patron saint." Donald Bennett was the flamboyant Colorado millionaire with a special love for Blanca Peak. He broadcast radio shows from the mountain's summit, made special phone calls to prominent people from atop Blanca using barb wire in place of phone lines —and he passionately believed in early surveys that incorrectly listed "his mountain" as the highest in Colorado—if not all of America.

Bitterly disappointed when more modern survey techniques reduced the height of Blanca Peak to fourth place among Colorado peaks, Bennett hired a crew of workers to pile rocks on top of the mountain to make up the 95 foot difference between Blanca and the first place mountain on the list, Mount Elbert. When this proved exceedingly difficult, Bennett arranged for a 50 foot aluminum flagpole to be placed on top of the rock pile. Its tip was long regarded as the highest point in Colorado.

As impressive as Blanca Peak is when viewed from the San Luis Valley, it is interesting to note that the bedrock floor of the San Luis Valley is actually below sea level, and present communities such as Alamosa are sitting atop 10,000 to 13,000 feet of accumulated sediment. Imagine what Blanca would look like when viewed from the original valley floor, some 10,000 to 13,000 feet lower!

MOUNT LINCOLN

BLANCA PEAK

More Crazy 14ers

One of the state's lowest 14ers is undoubtedly the most famous. Pikes Peak owes a portion of its fame to the annual motorized Pikes Peak Hill Climb. For the extremely fit, there's also a Pikes Peak Marathon. This annual endurance race to the top and back is a modern day version of a somewhat shorter 1950s era race that pitted teams of smokers against teams of non-smokers!

Mount Massive is Colorado's second highest peak, and as the name suggests, it is imposing. Due to an optical illusion, Mount Massive appears to be taller than Mount Elbert from most every vantage points. It is, in fact, 19 feet shorter.

In 1899, when the mines of 14er Mount Sneffels already had produced $35 million, it was proclaimed the "richest mountain in America." To this day, the mountain is a steady producer of precious metals. Sneffels is also one of Colorado's most photographed high peaks, perhaps because the main peak itself is surrounded by a rampart of 13 equally stunning peaks which approach, but don't quite attain, the 14,000 foot mark. These include Teakettle Mountain, Potosi Peak and Mount Kismet.

Surveyed in 1873, but not named until more than 50 years later, Mount Oxford was Colorado's forgotten 14er when "rediscovered" and finally given a name in 1925. Oxford was thought for years to be barely a 14er, somewhat like 14,001-foot Sunshine Peak. More careful measurements in the 1960s awarded Mount Oxford an additional 150 feet, boosting it from the state's 51st highest mountain to 27th. Other high mountains in Colorado have bounced above and below the magic 14,000 mark, with Mount of the Holy Cross being one peak that gained 14er status only in later years. The latest advance in mountain measurement technology is Global Positioning Systems (GPS), using satellites to precisely measure land features. A recent GPS survey of Mount Elbert, the state's highest mountain, increased the elevation from 14,433 feet to 14,440 feet.

Our fascination with "14ers" is lost on much of the rest of the world, where the metric system reigns supreme. In the European Alps, an even 4,000 meters is the magic number. There are 61 such mountains in the Alps. According to authors Gerry and Jennifer Roach writing in *Colorado's Thirteeners*, Spiller Peak in the San Juan Mountains is precisely 4000 meters (13,123 feet) tall. In all, the book lists a staggering 549 peaks in Colorado that qualify as 4,000ers! It is believed that no one person has climbed them all.

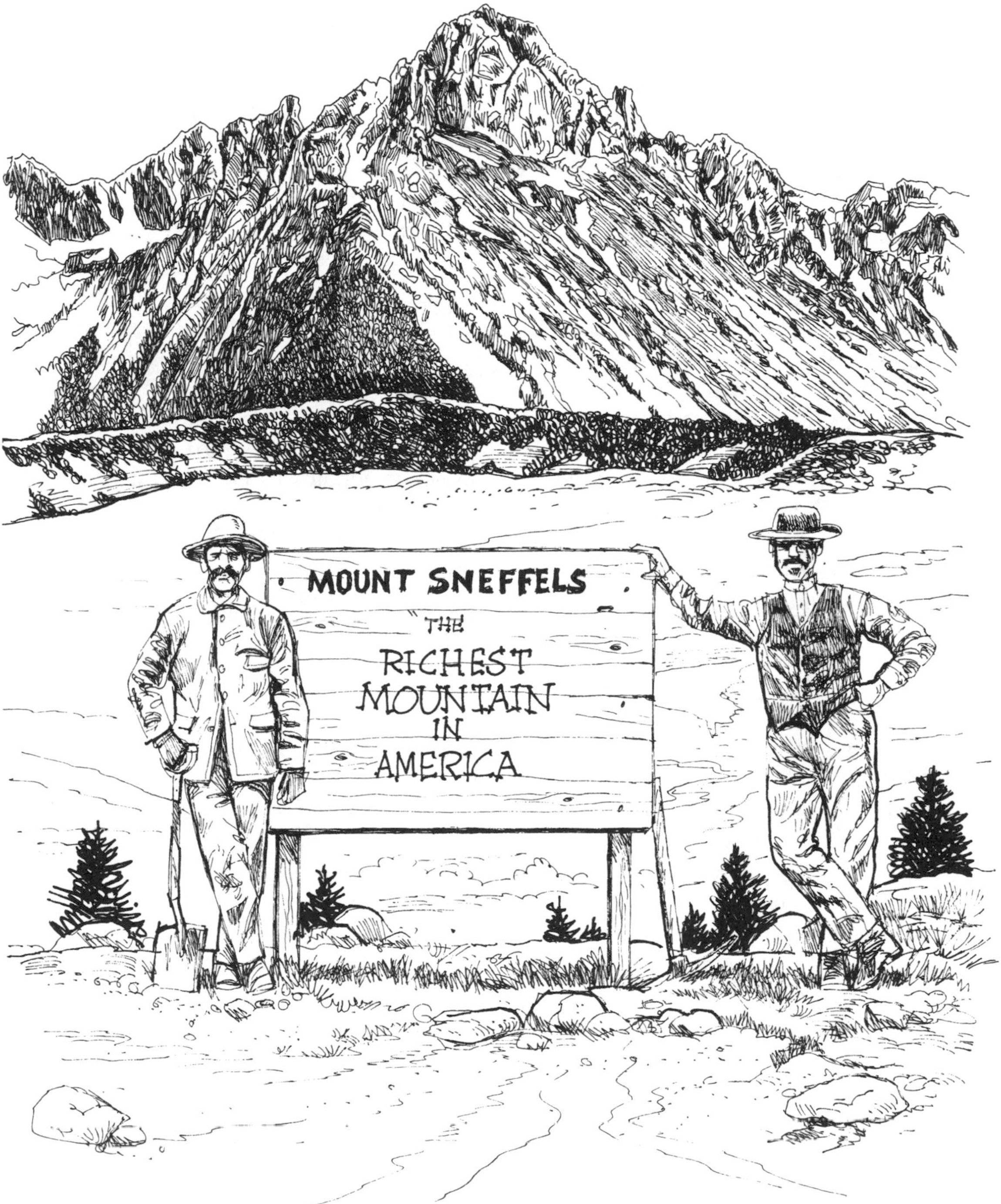
MOUNT SNEFFELS
"THE
RICHEST
MOUNTAIN
IN
AMERICA

Body Parts and Fake Cannons

The great westward migration on the Oregon, California and Mormon Trails rumbled just beyond Colorado's current northern border. After 1860, raiding Indians made travel dangerous on these trails through southeast Wyoming and the Nebraska Panhandle. Overland Stage Line responded by rerouting to the longer, but somewhat safer, "Overland" Trail from Julesburg down the South Platte to Denver — hence north to Laramie.

Julesburg was founded by Jules Beni, a surly and formidable French-Canadian who became an employee of Overland Stage. His boss was the even more notorious Jack Slade. The two men argued incessantly. Matters came to a head when Beni gunned down Slade — first with his six-shooter, then with two blasts from a shotgun. Beni told shocked bystanders to bury Slade in a dry goods box when he was dead. But Slade miraculously survived, his slow recovery fueled by revenge.

Slade eventually tracked Beni down, and killed him in an unhurried, brutal fashion. Afterwards he cut off both the victim's ears. Slade wore one ear ever after as a trophy on his watch chain. The other he nailed to a corral post at Virginia Dale. Named for Slade's wife Virginia, and located northwest of Fort Collins, Virginia Dale is the only surviving Overland Stage station on its original site.

Jack Slade was appointed station master at Virginia Dale in 1862. Ironically, he was also widely suspected of being in league with area outlaws, who always seemed to know when a stage departed, and precisely what valuables were onboard.

History largely ignored Slade. But in his time, Jack Slade was among the West's most intimidating characters. One of Slade's famous stagecoach guests at Virginia Dale was Mark Twain, who later wrote of having met this man who was "… more feared than God." Another guest was Schuyler Colfax, Speaker of the House and later the 17th vice president of the United States. Threats from hostile Indians detained Colfax at Virginia Dale for a week.

When Slade was fired by the Overland Stage Line, he drifted north to Virginia City, Montana. There his brash personality again put him in mortal danger. Vigilantes hung Slade not so much for crimes committed, as for crimes they were sure he would commit.

The next station master at Virginia Dale was "Colonel" Robert Spotswood who once ran a freighting business from Denver up and over 10,001 foot Kenosha Pass to Fairplay. On one trip across the pass, his ox team stampeded, throwing Spotswood and a lone passenger into a snow bank. The *Rocky Mountain News* reported the incident, and could not refrain from calling it the "Spotswood Oxpress."

As Virginia Dale's station master, Spotswood proved exceedingly ingenious. Once when hostile Indians approached the station, Spotswood found an old stove pipe, lashed it to the axle of a pair of wagon wheels, and rolled his contraption out the front door. When he began loading his pretend "cannon" with gunpowder, the Indians took it for the real thing, and promptly withdrew!

VIRGINIA DALE

Against All Odds

The histories of Colorado and New Mexico are inexorably linked. Both had been a Spanish territory since 1550. Together they were part of the Republic of Mexico, then the Republic of Texas. Colorado owed its first permanent non-Indian settlements to New Mexicans, when in 1851 Spanish-speaking residents of Taos and Santa Fe established communities just north of the present-day state border. In those years a good portion of southern Colorado was within New Mexico Territory.

Wild Bill Hickok, a man who by various accounts killed between 30 and 85 men, greatly enhanced his reputation by killing not a man, but a grizzly bear. It happened on Raton Pass, on the Colorado-New Mexico border. The year was 1860, and Hickok was driving stagecoaches over the Santa Fe Trail. He is reputed to have fought and killed the frothing grizzly on top of Raton Pass, armed only with a knife. In subsequent years Hickok would drift through New Mexico and Colorado Territories several times before his dramatic assassination in Deadwood, Dakota Territory, in 1876 (Author's note: see my *Black Hills Believables* for strange details of Hickok's death).

But the Wild West's most heroic defense against the odds wasn't by a familiar white figure such as Hickok, Wyatt Earp, or Buffalo Bill. No partner, this title belongs to a largely forgotten Hispanic deputy sheriff named Elfego Baca. In 1884, Baca had volunteered to disperse a gang of unruly cowboys from Texas, New Mexico and Colorado who were shooting up the little town of Frisco, New Mexico Territory. What he didn't expect to find was 80 heavily armed and ill-tempered cowpokes who eventually cornered Baca in a tiny adobe hut. During a period of 38 hours spanning parts of three days, his 80 assailants fired an estimated 4,000 rounds in Baca's direction. When finally rescued by fellow lawmen, Baca had survived without a scratch—and by some accounts had managed to kill four of his assailants while wounding eight others.

Once on safe ground, Baca had some explaining to do. He was accused of not being a duly sworn deputy sheriff, but instead acting on his own initiative and authority. His sheriff's "badge" was only a crude facsimile.

Was Elfego Baca a "good guy" or a "bad guy?" A court proceeding would decide.

One cowboy testified at trial that if he took a Colt .45 pistol, aimed it directly at Baca's chest from a foot away and fired, there would be absolutely no effect, as he believed that Baca was possessed of something "… from God or the devil." Maybe so. The door to the besieged adobe hut was taken into court as evidence, and that door alone contained 367 bullet holes! Baca was acquitted on grounds of self-defense.

ELFEGO BACA

The Mountain that Won a War

Massive Bartlett Mountain sits astride the Continental Divide north of Leadville. Here one finds the world's largest known deposit of molybdenum, a critical alloy that hardens steel and cast iron. This huge deposit isn't an outcropping on Bartlett Mountain; it *IS* Bartlett Mountain.

In 1959, the *Denver Post* used then-current estimates to declare that 85 percent of the world's molybdenum was contained in this one mountain. More recent estimates of world reserves has modified the claim to no more than one-third of world reserves, but it is true that at one time the Climax Mine on Bartlett Mountain produced three-quarters of the world's annual molybdenum output.

During the 19th century, prospectors crisscrossed Bartlett Mountain in a fruitless search for silver and gold. Those early miners had no way of knowing the true fortune beneath their feet. They eventually ignored the mountain, thinking its strange greasy metal to be a type of graphite. It wasn't until World War I that the military industrial complex recognized molybdenum as the alloy best suited to hardening steel for armaments. During World War II, the nations allied against Germany and Japan received almost all their needed molybdenum from the Climax Mine on Bartlett Mountain. Said the *Denver Post*, "From this one mountain came the wherewithal of winning wars . . . "

The Climax Mine eventually employed nearly 4,000 miners, and at one time was the world's largest underground mine. By some accounts this was the most successful American company of the Great Depression. Bartlett Mountain's mine may have been the sole source of a huge Allied demand for molybdenum during the World Wars, but by 1981 the mine was experiencing massive layoffs in the wake of a worldwide molybdenum market crash. Today the great mine stands empty. Bartlett, the mountain that won a war and made one company unimaginably wealthy, is once again just another mountain — ignored by today's unknowing motorists crossing Fremont Pass, just as it was by the prospectors of old.

Low Point in the Highest State

Elsewhere in this book you can read about the controversy over which of Colorado's lofty peaks is truly the highest. But who would have thought that a similar debate could develop about the state's lowest spot?

It all started in early 2000, when the *Rocky Mountain News* ran a little feature called *Wacky Questions*, to which Shirley Moran asked, "We all know that Mount Elbert is the highest point in Colorado, at 14,440 feet. But where is the lowest point in the state? How low?" The newspaper's answer? "It's in southeastern Colorado, along the banks of the Arkansas River, just west of the Kansas border. The elevation there is 3,350 feet." That seemed obvious, because for many years the Colorado Department of Transportation (CDoT) had perpetrated this myth by printing it on official highway maps.

It turns out that nobody had ever actually checked. *Rocky Mountain News* reader Dale Sanderson knew that CDoT had recently recanted on its "low point," moving it more than 100 miles north to a point where the North Fork of the Republican River leaves the state, elevation 3,337 feet. Sanderson was set to inform the newspaper editor of the new information, when he decided to consult detailed maps just to make sure this was, indeed, the state's lowest point. To his surprise, he found a still lower point further south, on the banks of the Arikaree River near the Colorado/Kansas/Nebraska tri-corner. The *Rocky Mountain News* graciously printed a correction, telling all that the new "low point" for the state was on the Arikaree River—elevation 3,315 feet. At about this time, Fred Anderson and others also had discovered the error. The U.S. Geological Survey even got into the act.

Who really cares about such wacky facts? Well, consider the world of High Pointing, the "sport" of attempting to reach the highest spot in all 50 states. Sometimes these high points are as unspectacular as a cattle feedlot in Iowa, or a suburban street corner in Delaware. In the yet more arcane pursuit of Low Pointing, individuals vie to reach the lowest point in each state. There is even a website, America's Basement, dedicated to Low Pointing.

Now we know Colorado's low point. Interestingly, the lowest point in our highest average-elevation state is still higher than the highest point in eighteen other states—higher than Pennsylvania's Mount Davis, higher than Arkansas' Magazine Mountain, and of course much higher than Florida's Britton Hill—elevation 345 feet and in last place among the states.

Colorado's Texas-Sized Bragging Rights

Colorado can't match Texas for size, but it does have some mighty impressive bragging rights relating to the "biggest," "best" or "most." Here is a sampler:

A huge stand of aspen trees on Kebler Pass west of Crested Butte is thought by some biologists to be the world's largest single organism. Because aspens propagate by sprouting from a common root system, the thousands upon thousands of interconnected aspens of the Kebler Pass grove do indeed share identical genetic makeup. Each fall the individual trees of this vast stand turn exactly the same shade of yellow/orange at precisely the same time.

North America's largest flat-topped mountain? Grand Mesa near Grand Junction is the biggest in North America—some say the world. The mesa is an ecologically distinct "island in the sky," rising nearly 7,000 feet above western Colorado's high desert, and the 60 by 30-mile topside of the mountain contains scores of lakes and lush evergreen forests. What's the state with the most land above 10,000 feet? No contest—Colorado has more than 75 percent of America's land area above 10,000 feet.

The highest military fort in the United States was Fort Peabody. This temporary fort was built by National Guardsmen in the winter of 1904 at a frigid 13,400-foot location. The fort, remnants of which are still visible, was intended to stop union sympathizers from entering Telluride via Imogene Pass. Though higher, the U.S. Army post once atop 14,110-foot Pikes Peak wasn't an armed fort as such, but served as a weather station.

Under the category of "once was, but no more," Denver's Colfax Avenue was for years the longest continuous street in America. Likewise, the biggest letter in the entire world was for a time the massive "W" at Western State College in Gunnison. It measures 400 feet by 350 feet.

Finally, there is this interesting theory, advanced by author Al Look in his book *Sidelights on Colorado*: If mountainous Colorado was "ironed out" to be as flat as a pancake, it would actually be bigger than Texas. Not so, according to *GeoWorld* magazine, which reported that even if the state's most mountainous county, San Juan County north of Durango, was stretched out to make it level, its land area would increase by slightly less than 10 percent.

Atomic Frenzy Grips Rockies

It was always Colorado's "other" yellow ore. But in time uranium would cause a stampede nearly as fervent as the Gold Rush of 100 years before.

Long before Europeans arrived in present-day Colorado, Indians knew about and gathered the soft golden mineral known today as uranium ore. It made for easily applied, bright yellow face paint! In those days, uranium ore could be found with relative ease in parts of the Western Slope.

As miners arrived, nearly all Indians were exiled to out-of-state reservations, and this peculiar yellow mineral was nearly forgotten. Forgotten, that is, until the early 1900s. That's when Madame Curie, a Polish-born French woman and first multiple recipient of a Nobel Prize, began her pioneering discoveries of radioactivity. Madame Curie needed uranium for her studies, and one of her sources was a mine near Paradox, Colorado. This uranium ore may have been destined for futuristic studies, but it was packed from mine to railhead on the backs of old-fashioned mules. Madame Curie is reputed to have subsequently visited Colorado to acquire still more uranium.

World War II's detonation of atomic bombs ushered in the true Atomic Age. Suddenly, uranium was in great demand. By the 1950s, Colorado's last great mineral rush was on—prospectors swarmed across the Four Corners area with their Geiger counters and army surplus jeeps. The U.S. government even guaranteed to buy all uranium production at a fixed price. Uranium was then thought of as the most strategic material ever found on American soil. Many believed that atomic power from uranium would provide everything from weapons for national security to all our electrical needs through nuclear generators, and even fuel for gas-free automobiles!

Sadly, miners who extracted uranium were exposed to as much as 750 times the safe levels of radiation. Hundreds of Four Corners uranium miners and their families succumbed to lung cancer, pulmonary fibrosis and birth defects before the government stepped in to mandate mine ventilation and safety standards.

In the 1920s, Madame Curie had paid the princely sum of $120,000 for a single gram of pure Colorado radium, a byproduct of uranium ore. Prices would go even higher in the coming decades. In a great irony of history, Colorado's early gold and silver miners were routinely penalized at reduction mills for bringing in ore that contained "worthless" uranium.

Madame Curie

Arkansas River Divided Nations!

During the 1930s, it was discovered that portions of Summit and Grand Counties had been left off old treaty maps through a cartographer's error. Was it possible that a 2,700 square-mile chunk of the Centennial State hadn't been properly incorporated into the Union?

To explain this bizarre story, we must go back in time to when the Arkansas River was an international border. It all started with Pope Alexander VI, who mandated through the Treaty of Tordesillos that Spain could rule the New World west of the Mississippi River. As time passed, the French had other ideas, and soon French trappers and traders were drifting southwest from the Mississippi to establish posts in what's now northern Colorado.

From outposts in Taos and Santa Fe, the Spaniards similarly eased into present-day southern Colorado. So it was that the Arkansas River became a sort of informal boundary between New Spain and New France. This division is echoed in today's place names—north of the Arkansas, one finds the French language at La Porte, La Salle, Cache la Poudre River and St. Vrain. Even the Platte River, where "Platte" means flat or shallow, reflects the influence of the French and their language. But at or below the Arkansas, one sees a decidedly Spanish influence with names like Alamosa, Pueblo, Cortez, Durango, Trinidad, and the San Luis Valley.

When Napoleon gained formal control of Louisiana Territory in 1802, he promptly sold it to the fledgling United States. It was clear to all that Louisiana Territory included the watershed of the mighty Missouri River, and most of present day Colorado east of the Great Divide. What was unclear was the exact border between this larger version of the United States and New Spain. Partial clarification came with the Transcontinental Treaty of 1819, which proclaimed the border to be the Arkansas River. Thus, the river would be the official border between Spain and America for several years, after which it became the border with newly independent Mexico. In 1848, at the conclusion of the Mexican War, the border was shifted south to the Rio Grande.

When renowned Bent's Fort and trading post was established on the Santa Fe Trail in 1833, the Bent brothers carefully chose a site on the *north* bank of the Arkansas, the American bank. This meant fewer regulations, and less chance of being influenced by strict Mexican authorities in Santa Fe.

What if the Arkansas was still an international border? Colorado would have "border" towns—places like La Junta, Lamar, Florence and Salida would be on the Mexican side. Pueblo would be divided almost precisely in half, with sections north of the river in the United States, and those portions south in Mexico. Such was the case in 1842, when Pueblo first came into existence. Back then the dusty little village was known as El Pueblo. Later dubbed the "Cultural Crossroads of the Arkansas," El Pueblo was a roughshod mix of Yankees, Indians, Mexicans, Frenchmen and African-Americans.

Because one could simply wade across the river and be in a different country, El Pueblo tended to attract a less than desirable element—fugitives of justice from either the United States or Mexico—men who were comforted by having a river-border as a handy escape route.

But what about that unclaimed territory in the heart of Colorado and the nation? For that, turn to the next story.

Charles Bent

AMERICA

SITE OF
BENT'S FORT

ARKANSAS RIVER

MEXICO

William Bent

No Man's Land

During the Great Depression, a 90-by 30-mile swath of Summit and Grand Counties was discovered to have been left off treaty maps. It was, some would say, unclaimed territory resulting from centuries-old land claims for what is now Colorado by the Spanish, French, Mexicans, Texans and eventually the United States.

This curious situation stems from the 1819 Transcontinental Treaty, meant to settle the fuzzy boundary between New Spain and America's newly acquired Louisiana Purchase. This treaty declared the Arkansas River as border, all the way to its headwaters at Fremont Pass near Climax.

From the headwaters, the border was established as a straight line due north for 200 miles. Everything west of that line would belong to Spain—everything east of the Continental Divide already belonged to the United States by way of the Louisiana Purchase. The problem was, in 1819 no one knew the whereabouts of the headwaters of the Arkansas River! Thus, the treaty wording inadvertently created a large gap west of the Divide, but east of the treaty line, which could be interpreted as belonging to no country! This was to become the infamous No Man's Land, site of many modern locations of note: Breckenridge, Granby, Winter Park, Dillon, and Keystone.

For a few unsettling weeks in 1936, some residents of Breckenridge believed the "missing" 2,700 square miles of Colorado had never been properly annexed by the United States. The Breckenridge Women's Club caught wind of the error, and took it on as a cause, marching down to Denver and the governor's office. Club members pointed out the historical error to the governor, and demanded action!

Perhaps because he was then campaigning for a U.S. Senate seat, Governor Edwin Johnson agreed to participate in a ceremony claiming the land for the United States. So it came to pass that on August 8, 1936, a flag-raising was held on the lawn of the Summit County Court House. Presiding were Governor Johnson and other dignitaries. In attendance were hundreds of spectators and a brass band. The event was beamed live across the country and to some foreign lands via a radio remote broadcast.

As the years passed, an urban legend developed that Breckenridge could have been its own little country—thus the moniker "Kingdom of Breckenridge," which is used to this day. For more than 30 years, Breckenridge celebrated its lost territory status in an August event known as No Man's Land Festival. Experts in international law are nearly unanimous in stating that present-day Summit and Grand counties were never actually lands without a country. Yet one can still find the occasional old-timer in this former No Man's Land who harkens back to the years before 1936, and would beg to differ.

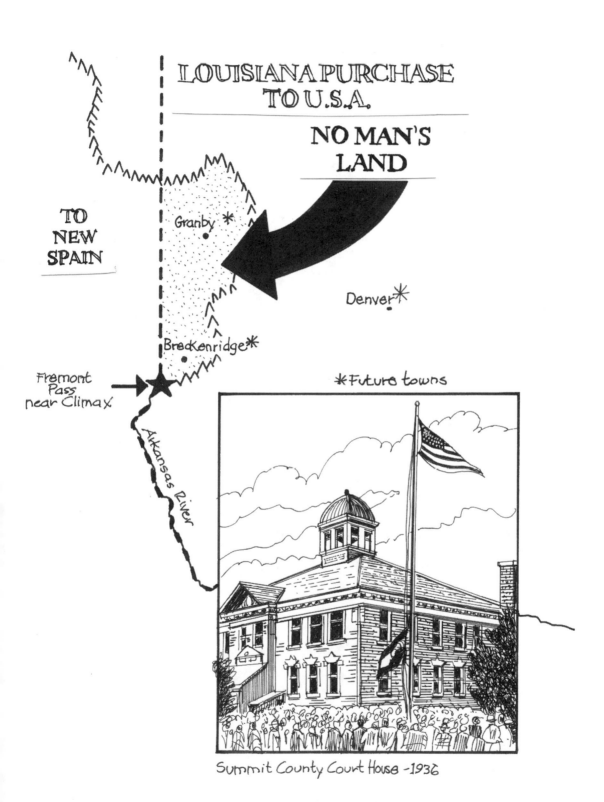

LOUISIANA PURCHASE
TO U.S.A.

NO MAN'S
LAND

TO
NEW
SPAIN

Granby *

Denver *

Breckenridge *

Fremont
Pass
near Climax

Arkansas River

*Future towns

Summit County Court House -1936

Wind and Water Solve Dunes Mystery

Author Hal Clifford calls the Great Sand Dunes one of the five natural wonders of Colorado. And no wonder. At more than 700 feet in height, these are the tallest sand dunes in North America. The 39 square miles of the Great Sand Dunes contain at least five billion cubic yards of perfectly uniform sand. The sand is really bits and pieces of the San Juan Mountains to the west, some of it eroded particles of rock left by alpine glaciers in the Ice Age, and all of it carried into the San Luis Valley by the Rio Grande.

The San Luis Valley is a true desert, with parts receiving less than eight inches of precipitation annually. In this environment, prevailing winds from the southwest push and bounce the dry sand eastward toward the imposing Sangre de Cristo Mountains. Seeking a route over these barrier mountains, the wind funnels through three low mountain passes just east of the Great Sand Dunes. As winds slow down slightly on the uphill surge, the heavier sand-sized particles are dropped, and the result is the Great Sand Dunes.

But why doesn't the prevailing wind move the dunes inexorably eastward until they bump into the mountains? Ah, the secret of the arid San Luis Valley's Great Sand Dunes is not the wind, but rather the water! Medano Creek flanks the eastern edge of the dunes. As the dunes relentlessly advance to the east, they collapse into Medano Creek, which carries sand back to the west before disappearing into the porous soils of the valley. Here the wind picks up the same sand particles, and tumbles them right back to the dunes. This constant recycling of sand is the main reason behind the historic stability of these dunes.

In addition, small streams and passing storms contribute more water, which flows directly under and into the dunes. Thus, while the top few feet of the dunes are dry and hot (often 140 degrees Fahrenheit!), most of each dune is wet and thus more stable.

The National Park Service encourages visitors to climb all over the dunes, knowing that footprints left today will be "gone with the wind" tomorrow. Billions of tiny grains of sand are constantly making the same round trip from west to east, and back west again, insuring that Colorado's Great Sand Dunes are always changing, yet always the same!

Native Notes and Drumbeats

Bow-and-arrow technology arrived in present-day Colorado around 400 A.D. Any "arrowhead" you find older than this is more properly called a projectile point—the tip of a spear. Even after acquiring guns, some Indians preferred the bow and arrow. Unlike guns, a bow and arrow never jammed, was comparatively quiet, created a more deadly wound. And a skilled native archer could launch many more arrows than bullets per minute.

Utes and other Colorado Indian tribes knew the location of many hot springs. They occasionally enjoyed a warm, therapeutic soak. And with the advent of horses, they also learned that the best way to treat a lame horse was to ride the steed right into a hot springs, there to soak for a good long time.

The Colorado Mountain Club and other organizations may feel they have accurately chronicled the first ascents of Colorado's 14ers—and many of its 13,000 foot peaks as well. But it's a certainty that those 19th and 20th century achievements weren't "firsts" at all—Native Americans had climbed to the top of most notable Rocky Mountain peaks long before Columbus landed in the New World!

These native mountaineers reached summits without climbing equipment and without modern clothing. They climbed for reasons we know and reasons we don't know. They climbed to build stone eagle traps to acquire treasured ceremonial eagle feathers. They climbed to find deeper meaning through vision quests. Sometimes they climbed to pursue game animals, which in summer often seek the tundra's cool slopes and tender vegetation. In *Ways to the Sky: A Historical Guide to North American Mountaineering*, Andy Selters is perhaps the first author to fully acknowledge these unrecorded ascents by native people.

White buffalo hunters of the 19th century learned some of their best tricks from the Indians. Here's one that worked during cooler weather: Ride into an area where one hopes to find buffalo. Pitch camp and go to sleep. Upon rising, scan the horizon for a vapor cloud. This is the condensed breath of thousands of buffalo!

Hunters and earlier mountain men also learned utilitarian ways of dressing from the Indians. For example, what we think of as the ornamentation of fringed leather coats and pants was primarily a practical matter. During rain storms, the fringe encourages water to drip off instead of soaking into the leather clothing.

In 1835, Colonel Henry Dodge led 120 mounted Dragoons in an expedition westward to the Rockies. His mission was to encourage traditionally warring tribes to peacefully coexist. Upon reaching present day Weld County, Colorado, Dodge and his men camped with the Cheyenne tribe. From this camp they were startled by an advancing tribe of Pawnee, firing their 100 guns into the air, volley after volley. Supposing this barrage to be an attack, Dodge ordered preparation for battle. But in fact, the gunfire was a peace offering; the Pawnee only intended to prove their friendliness by approaching with empty guns!

Ute Chief
Ouray

Mystery Shrouds Mount of the Holy Cross

One of the enduring enigmas of the Old West was a rumored huge cross on a remote Colorado peak. It was a mystery that seemed like just another mountain man's tall tale—that is, until 1873.

That's the year when frontier photographer William Jackson promised his bride-to-be that he'd find and photograph the Cross, if it existed, as his wedding gift to her.

Jackson and a group of surveyors began their search armed only with "hearsay" directions. In a stroke of luck, the party stumbled upon a large encampment of Indians led by the great Ute chief Ouray. Ouray remembered seeing the Cross, and agreed to guide Jackson part way there.

Once in the vicinity, Jackson determined that the Cross could be photographed only by summiting 13,003-foot Notch Mountain. Misty weather made for a less than ideal photo opportunity. But finally, on August 23rd, thick clouds parted long enough for a clear view across the mountaintops. Jackson's resulting print proved the Holy Cross existed, and it instantly became one of the most famous photographs of the Nineteenth Century.

This "Cross of Snow" was an imposing sight. The vertical axis towered nearly 1,500 feet. The horizontal arms reached 700 feet from tip to tip.

Newspapers across the country reprinted Jackson's "discovery" photo. The following year, noted artist Thomas Moran retraced Jackson's footsteps, and his painting of the mountain became nearly as famous as the photo. Henry Longfellow joined in, penning the following verse:

"There is a mountain in the distant West
That, sun-defying, in its deep ravines
Displays a cross of snow upon its side."

Jackson would live to see the Mount of the Holy Cross declared a National Monument by President Herbert Hoover.

But the Monument, located in an inaccessible region, would in some months of the year attract nary a single visitor! The Monument's superintendent conceded, "It involves a climb worth half your life to get up Notch Mountain where you can see the Cross."

In 1950, the *Denver Post* published an aerial photo of the peak with a headline which asked, "Is Cross Fading?" Some claimed the right arm of the cross had deteriorated. And so it was that Congress passed bill No.73339, which read, in part, "The purpose of this bill is to abolish the Holy Cross National Monument. The right arm of the cross is not now as sharply defined as it once was."

Then, as now, the peak stood in controversy. Did Jackson retouch his famous photo to enhance the effect of the Cross? Modern evidence suggests he probably did—at least a little. And the mountain wasn't even considered a l4er until 1964. Until then, the Geological Survey listing was four feet short at 13,996 feet. Re-measured, the Mount was found to be nine feet taller, and thus became the second shortest of Colorado's 54 "l4ers."

Yet the mountain's champions aren't fazed by monument status, retouching controversy or "l4er" status. Mount of the Holy Cross always has, and always will, attract followers...and a reputation for the miraculous.

From the mid-1920s through the 1930s, as many as 2,000 religious pilgrims annually trekked to the Bowl of Tears, a small lake at foot of the Cross. Here baptisms were held. And thousands of handkerchiefs sent from all over the world would be dipped in

the Bowl of Tears. Sick people believed that the handkerchiefs, thus blessed, would cure them.

Rumors of a curse on miners who extracted minerals from the Holy Cross district contrast sharply with more benevolent or even "miraculous" events. Here are two of many: In 1968, a 16-year-old boy became separated from his party in a driving hail storm above timberline. For two weeks he was missing, and presumed dead, but was eventually found alive and no worse for wear—on the slopes of the Holy Cross. As recently as 1997, a disoriented 67-year-old Kathleen Kinderfather surprised many by surviving cool, wet weather for five days and nights on the boulder fields of the Mount of the Holy Cross.

The mountain has blessed many, including Jackson. One month after his "discovery," Jackson presented the famous print to his fiancée...and then married her. Longfellow's connection with the Cross isn't as happy. Read on to find the true topic of his poem—a poet's distant but still painful loss of a loving wife:

"There is a mountain in the distant West
That, sun-defying, in its deep ravines
Displays a cross of snow upon its side.
Such is the cross I bear upon my breast
These eighteen years, through all the chang-
ing scenes
And seasons, changeless since the day she
died."

44 Tales Too Good to Leave Out

1 Back in 1899, banker J.P. Morgan funded a plan to communicate with extra-terrestrials by beaming radio signals into space from a big backyard coil of wire in Colorado Springs. This project, brainchild of inventor Nikoli Tesla, was one of history's first attempts to communicate with life on Mars and other heavenly bodies. The transformer is said to have made the neighbor's hair stand on end!

2 In May 1898, Coloradoans responded to the Spanish American War by assembling a cavalry of fightin' cowboys known as "Torrey's Rough Riders." These men and horses, bound for Cuba, got only as far as Jacksonville, Florida, so the Coloradoans never saw action. Teddy Roosevelt's Rough Riders got to San Juan Hill first, and the rest is history!

3 In 1880, a certain pioneer crossed the mighty San Juan Mountains of southwestern Colorado with a sheet iron stove strapped to his back. The plan was to reach Durango and start a restaurant that would nourish prospectors then flocking to the area. His name was John Elitch. His restaurant was soon a success, but by 1888 Elitch had returned to Denver to start the famous Elitch Gardens. It would grow to be the largest amusement park in the Rocky Mountain region!

4 By 1950, the narrow gauge D&RGW railroad was losing money, and petitioned the transportation commission to cease operations. But the harder the railroad tried to close the Durango to Silverton line, the more people climbed aboard to enjoy "one last ride." Today the D&RGW is America's favorite historic train ride. In the 1970s, a friend of a D&RGW engineer boasted that he could peddle his bike to Silverton faster than the steam engine could chug-a-chug up there. Bets were placed, and the biker won—just barely. Thus, the annual Iron Horse bicycle challenge was born. Every year in May, some bikers beat the train—and some don't.

5 Sixty years ago, a Grand Junction high school baseball game was tied in the late innings. When a left-handed batter knocked a home run, he ran the bases the wrong way. After some thought, the umpire decided this unorthodox base running had "untied" the score, and he awarded the victory to the other team!

6 Among the strangest ways of getting from the "civilized" eastern states to Colorado was the wind wagon. In the late 1880s, one such wagon is said to have covered 50 miles in a single day! Normally, however, prevailing winds are uncooperatively out of the northwest, not the east. Another curious mode of frontier transportation was a bicycle with the five-foot front wheel and the tiny back wheel. One fellow rode such a contraption all the way from Missouri to Denver!

7 How far does a golf ball fly at 9,324 feet? According to promoters of Breckenridge's golf courses, the thin air at that elevation does allow for less resistance against your golf ball. Most players can anticipate an increase in the distance they hit the ball. As a general rule, it is suggested high ball hitters will see about a 20 percent increase, while lower ball flight players can expect only a 10 percent gain.

8 One hundred years ago, the editor of a Montana newspaper was riding the high trails above Telluride when he reported something strange on the roof of a house of prostitution. The multi-colored shingles were arranged in such a way as to suggest an enticing woman, apparently a subtle advertisement meant for miners coming down from the mines!

9 The Teflon-coated fiberglass roof of Denver International Airport is the largest fully integrated roof in the world.

10 Technically, Colorado Territory was opened to slavery by the Supreme Court's Dred Scott Decision of 1857. Then came Abe Lincoln's 1863 Emancipation Proclamation. The Proclamation did little for hapless Indians in Colorado's southern San Luis Valley, who were routinely bought and sold in a hush-hush slave trade. And as late as 1876, the year Colorado became a state, an African-American male was allegedly sold into slavery in Leadville to pay off a gambling debt!

11 The old McNichols Sports Arena was built to host Olympic figure skating and hockey, because it was believed that Denver would be awarded the 1976 Olympic Games. The Games were indeed awarded to Colorado, which then became the only U.S. state to vote against hosting the Games. Innsbruck, Austria, became the substitute Olympic host.

12 One of Denver's first rodeos was held without benefit of fences. People simply crowded around the "arena" — that is, until one bucking bronco broke loose and caused injuries and general mayhem among spectators.

13 In 1942, empty prairie near Granada was transformed overnight into the largest community in southeast Colorado. Unfortunately, the "town" of Amache was really a detainment camp for Japanese-Americans, complete with barb wire and guard towers. Two-thirds of the camp's 7,620 detainees were native-born American citizens, but virtually all Japanese-Americans on the West Coast were forcibly removed by President Roosevelt's Executive Order 9066 to camps in remote areas. Detainees were forced to sell nearly all personal property, sometimes at a huge loss.

When construction of a high school for Amache detainees was proposed, editorials in the *Denver Post* and other newspapers gave voice to those who felt this was money spent to "... coddle people sympathetic to the enemy." However, Amache High School was built, and even fielded a football team for one remarkable game within the fences of the detainment camp. The game, against nearby Holly High School, was purposely planned for Armistice Day of 1943. Amache won 7-0. Plans for a similar game against Wiley High School the following year were cancelled by anti-Japanese sentiment. But when young men from Amache Camp were shortly allowed to join the armed forces, many volunteered for combat duty and served America with distinction.

14 Unaweep Canyon near Gateway may be the world's most geologically unique canyon. This long, deep canyon has two mouths, not one, situated at opposite ends of its 40 mile length. Equally weird is Paradox Valley. Invariably, a valley parallels a stream or river. But in this case, the Dolores River crosses the valley on the short axis, hence the "paradox." This phenomenon is the result of the collapse of a huge salt dome, and is best witnessed from the little hamlet of Bedrock.

15 So uncompromisingly alpine are Colorado counties like San Juan (Silverton) and Hinsdale (Lake City), that there are some years when the Bureau of Statistics can't find one acre of agricultural land. These two counties have only a few hundred year-round residents each. Thus, a motor vehicle fatality, or two, can instantly transform either from safest place in the nation to the least safe. Likewise, just a few persons losing their job can rocket the unemployment rate from among the nation's lowest, to among the nation's highest—statistically, that is!

16 Colorado's Weld County is a darn big county. At roughly 4,000 square miles, Weld County is more than three times bigger than Rhode Island, about twice as big as Delaware and four-fifths the size of Connecticut.

17 In their native tongue, many tribes greeted the arrival of the horse by calling it "Big Dog." The Comanche called this new creature "God's Dog." Life with horses meant many good things for the nomadic Plains Indian. More spacious teepees could be transported. Children could get a free ride instead of being carried or forced to walk. And the elderly enjoyed much longer lives, because before horses, walking long distances was a prerequisite of nomadic life. Before horses, an elderly person understood what would happen when he or she could no longer "keep up" in pursuit of game herds—in what was often a mutual decision, the elder would remain behind to perish.

18 The state stone of Colorado is the aquamarine. You might find one right on top of Mount Antero, the 14,269 foot peak near Salida that is easily North America's highest gemstone collecting site.

19 Walk through Grandview Cemetery in Fort Collins and one will eventually come across a headstone that may startle the historically literate: Haile Selassie! Wasn't this the emperor of Ethiopia, idolized by countrymen for decades and even worshipped as a god by Rastafarians? Actually, this is his son, Haile G. Selassie, an engineer who attended Colorado State University for a time, and who died far from African soil on November 27, 1990. Another notable Colorado tombstone is found in Mt. Pisgah cemetery in Cripple Creek, where the epitaph reads "He Called Bill Smith a Liar."

20 Denver's Daniels and Fisher Tower, at 372 feet tall, was at one time the third tallest building in the United States. It was modeled after the campanile of St. Mark's in Venice, Italy.

21 The next time you visit the Great Sand Dunes National Park, consider a side trip to an underground waterfall that few visitors even know about. Zapata Falls is accessible by gravel road on Bureau of Land Management land four miles east of Colorado Highway 150, just south of the entrance to the National Park. The falls are hidden deep in a cave, and are often completely frozen in a stunning aqua-blue. Be prepared to approach the falls by walking on ice, except in summer.

22 What was the biggest nugget ever mined in Colorado? Some sources say it was a 1,840 pound silver nugget taken from the Molly Gibson Mine near Aspen. Others say it was a 2,350 pounder, also of silver, discovered in the Smuggler Mine. Either way, a nugget the weight of a small car is a big nugget—so big that each had to be broken up so the mine shaft elevator could lug the treasure to the surface.

23 There are more deaths by avalanche in Colorado than in any other state. People underestimate the sheer power of an avalanche. A cubic yard of Colorado spring snow, when packed, can weigh half a ton! So when several hundred thousand cubic yards of snow begin moving downhill, it is an unstoppable force. Watch for the many treeless avalanche chutes in the San Juans and elsewhere. In Ouray, local folks even have names for the prominent chutes perched above their homes

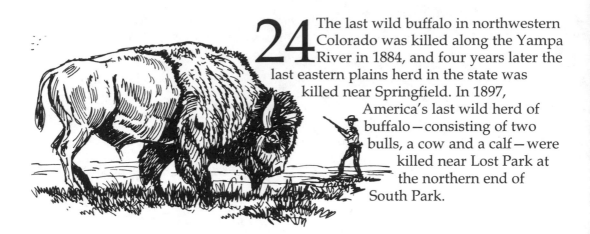

24 The last wild buffalo in northwestern Colorado was killed along the Yampa River in 1884, and four years later the last eastern plains herd in the state was killed near Springfield. In 1897, America's last wild herd of buffalo—consisting of two bulls, a cow and a calf—were killed near Lost Park at the northern end of South Park.

25 Colorado has its share of rattlesnakes. On one terrifying day on the plains of eastern Colorado, a woman ever-after known as Rattlesnake Kate found herself surrounded by snakes coming out of hibernation. She is reputed to have killed 140 of the creatures, and then made a dress out of their skins.

26 There is tantalizing evidence that Coors Field is built on the site of a long-ago buffalo jump, where Indians harvested buffalo by either stampeding them off a bluff, or corralling them for easy slaughter in what archaeologists call an arroyo trap.

27 Lewis and Clark never set foot in what's now Colorado. But in 1776, almost 30 years ahead of the more famous duo, Father Escalante and Father Dominguez set out from Santa Fe on an eerily similar mission—to find an overland route to the Pacific and Monterey, California. They traveled through southwest Colorado, naming many rivers and landmarks along the way. While camped on the Dolores River, Dominguez found the ancient cliff ruins of a small Indian village, which Escalante noted in his journal. This was the first written record of a prehistoric Anasazi site in Colorado. The site is now called Escalante Ruin. Traveling a circuitous 2,000 miles through the Great Basin, the explorers were admittedly lost much of the time. They were ultimately turned back by weather and dwindling supplies near the present Utah-Nevada border—well short of their goal of the Pacific Ocean.

28 A legend of the Arapaho tribe spoke of a mesa, near Golden, which the Great Maker had deemed a forbidden land. It is said members of the tribe could ride up to the edge of the mesa, but never dared venture on to it.

29 Red Rocks has been called the most acoustically perfect natural amphitheater in the world.

30 Robert H. Latta arrived in Colorado in 1881, and later provided this interesting entry in his brief autobiography: "I was in Cripple Creek on business. One evening I saw a crowd of miners, led by a brass band, playing "There'll Be a Hot Time in the Old Town Tonight," making the rounds of the saloons. They were "celebrating" the funeral of one of their friends, and were carrying his coffin with them. Laughing and shouting, they followed the band from one saloon to the next all the way down the street, stopping each time for a drink in honor of the deceased. It was the noisiest funeral party I ever saw."

Also from Robert Latta's recollections is this passage: "The Circle Railroad had a station the other side of Cherry Creek on Larimer Street. They had a small engine and a few cars. The road ran through South Denver. One day a train killed a man. Soon after, the train broke into the station without the engineer or fireman on it. It was said that both of them saw the ghost of the dead man on the track, got scared and jumped from the engine, letting it go wild."

31 In an equally eerie train story from the 1890s, the crew of a night train bound for Cripple Creek reported that the locomotive's lights briefly illuminated a man walking beside the tracks in prison garb. His prison number was clearly visible. Upon reaching the next station, the engineer reported the sighting to nearby Colorado State Penitentiary in Canon City, only to be informed that the number in question belonged to a prisoner who had been executed some days before. Then as now, the site of the incident is known as Phantom Canyon. The narrow gauge railroad is long gone, but you may still drive Phantom Canyon Road in your car.

32 Here are a few items from the ski trivia file: The first fatality of commercial skiing in Colorado was Berrieu Hughes, who died at Loveland Pass in May 1939. The popular "Hughes" ski run at Winter Park is named in his honor. Buddy Werner is remembered as America's first world-class alpine ski racer. He lived in Steamboat Springs, but died in the Swiss Alps trying to outrace an avalanche while filming a documentary. Before his death, the ski mountain at Steamboat was known as Storm Mountain. Now it is called Mount Werner. Copper Mountain Ski Area was envisioned and designed as the alpine ski venue for the 1976 Winter Olympics. The '76 Games were formally awarded to Colorado, but state citizens had the final say, and they voted "no" because of concerns about cost, pollution and crowding. When Salida Mayor Mike Ferno stepped in to make sure the Monarch Ski Area had a lodge, folks didn't have to think long for a name: Inn Ferno!

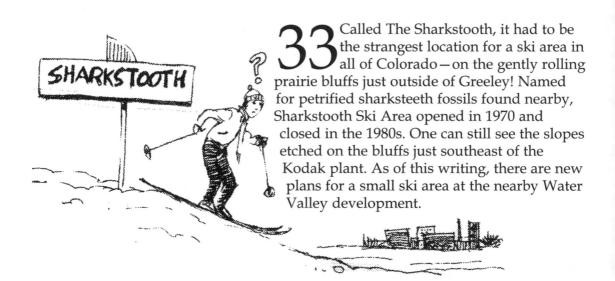

33 Called The Sharkstooth, it had to be the strangest location for a ski area in all of Colorado—on the gently rolling prairie bluffs just outside of Greeley! Named for petrified sharksteeth fossils found nearby, Sharkstooth Ski Area opened in 1970 and closed in the 1980s. One can still see the slopes etched on the bluffs just southeast of the Kodak plant. As of this writing, there are new plans for a small ski area at the nearby Water Valley development.

34 An earlier chapter in this book sheds light on the Colorado saga of one Alferd Packer, the only American ever tried and convicted of cannibalism. To the amusement of many, the 1968 student body at the University of Colorado in Boulder christened their new cafeteria The Alferd E. Packer Memorial Grill! Later a statue "honoring" Packer was placed on the Boulder campus.

35 Texans have a long history of vacationing in Colorado's mountains. So it may come as no surprise that the envious Lone Star State once planned to buy land in the Centennial State to establish a Texas State Park!

36 Charles Lindbergh may have been the first aviator to conduct aerial photography of an archaeological site on a flight over Mesa Verde. It was the late 1920s, and his flight uncovered some of the more remote ruins.

37 The vast Sand Hills of Nebraska, Kansas and Colorado are stabilized by grass. Jim Swinehart, a scientist with the University of Nebraska, has asked a disturbing question: What would happen if a prolonged drought, a drought worse than the Dust Bowl of the 1930s, were to occur? Geologists believe that as recently as 900 years ago, the Sand Hills were pure sand—no stabilizing grass, resulting in periods called "dune time," a time when winds caused the lifeless dunes to march slowly across the land. Though Swinehart will not guess as to when "dune time" will come again, he's sure one day another super drought will set the ocean of sand in motion.

38 The presumed largest blue spruce in the world is on Gunnison National Forest land near West Elk Creek and north of Blue Mesa Reservoir. If you go looking for it, take a tape measure. This giant tree is 15.8 feet in circumference and 124 feet tall. But rival state Utah uncovered an even bigger blue spruce. See page 135 for more on this.

39 Zebulon Pike is best remembered for his namesake peak, but also for his military service in exploration of present-day Colorado. It is interesting to speculate on a rather bizarre claim made by a minority of historians—that Pike was doubling as a spy for a group of men, including Aaron Burr and James Wilkinson, who hoped to start a new nation between the United States and New Spain. In 1805, General James Wilkinson was appointed to govern the huge Louisiana Purchase. He sent Pike westward, ostensibly to locate the headwaters of the Red River and thus establish the extent of the new Louisiana Purchase, but some say his real mission was to gather intelligence on Spanish military operations.

Pike was captured by the Spaniards, who may have mistaken Pike's star charts for spy documents. Pike is said to have refused their offer to be escorted to the Red River and released. Instead, Pike allowed himself and his men to be taken into custody and escorted to Santa Fe, and eventually Chihuahua. It was, say conspiracy theorists, Pike's perfect opportunity to observe the size and placement of the Spanish Army. Noted historian William Goetzmann has called Pike's expedition, "… the most successful espionage operation in American history."

40 In 1973, novelist Stephen King moved to a rented house in Boulder. While seeking fodder for a new novel, he checked into the historic and some say haunted Stanley Hotel in Estes Park. He stayed in Room 217, and while there was inspired to write of a family hired as winter caretakers of a vast, snowbound hotel. The tale became his third best-selling novel, *The Shining*, which in turn was made into a hit movie starring Jack Nicholson.

41 The famous 10th Mountain Division, those World War II soldiers on skis, trained at Camp Hale north of Leadville. Robert Dole, former Senator and 1996 presidential candidate, was a member of the division. Of those 10th Mountain veterans who survived combat in the Aleutian Islands and Italy, a group went on to construct, own or manage nearly 60 ski areas across the United States. If you'd like to ski the same slopes where 8,000 troopers of the famed 10th learned to ski, buy a lift ticket at cozy Ski Cooper.

42 In 1869, Wyoming sent shock waves across America by becoming the first state to give women the vote. This was more than fifty years before national suffrage was achieved. Was it a publicity stunt to attract more settlers? A panicked effort to counteract the votes of newly enfranchised African-American men in western territories? Susan B. Anthony encouraged eastern women to migrate en masse to Wyoming. Colorado joined Wyoming in extending the vote to women in 1893. Organizers in Colorado used the following amusing but effective campaign slogan: "Let the women vote! They can't do any worse than the men have!"

43 Among the northernmost of Colorado's great mountain ranges is the Mummy Range, so named because one early visitor thought this group of mountains looked like an Egyptian mummy. Two peaks of the range, located at the north end of Rocky Mountain National Park, tower more than 13,500 feet. Heavy winter snows collect in vast snow fields that persist year-round. You may prefer the aboriginal name inspired by the eternal snows (especially if you, like many, find it impossible to see a "mummy")—the Arapaho people called these mountains the Snowy Owls.

44 Colorado is not noted for having especially big trees, but we do have a few giants. The biggest plains cottonwood in the world is right here. It is 105 feet tall, with a 115-foot wide crown. The tree's trunk is 36 feet in circumference! The next time you're in tiny Hygiene, just west of Longmont, keep an eye out for this giant, or ask a local for directions. Our state's tallest ponderosa pine is impressive. It grows somewhere in the San Juan Mountains, and is 160 feet tall. The people who keep track of such things are at **http://coloradotrees.org/champions/**. Check the site for lists of hundreds of big trees. You might even find a state champion lurking in your own backyard, for some of the state champs are not so imposing--take the current Colorado state champion paperbark maple. It's just 15 feet tall.

Index

139

Notes